Belinda Davidson is an international speaker, bestselling author and spiritual mentor.

For fifteen years, Belinda worked as a professional medical intuitive, working closely with doctors and healthcare practitioners, and for over twenty years she's worked as a spiritual coach and mentor. Her clients include celebrities, CEOs and well-known business and industry leaders.

Belinda was born highly intuitive and very psychic. 'A curse in her childhood,' she says, 'a wonderful gift later in life.'

To find out more about Belinda visit: belindadavidson.com.

BELINDA DAVIDSON

FIND YOUR LIGHT

How to heal your shadow and your life

MACMILLAN

Pan Macmillan Australia

To Jean and Tanya

CONTENTS

INTRODUCTION

I was born exceptionally psychic. For as long as I can remember, I've been able to find out all about a person by looking inside and around their bodies and reading their 'inner light' and chakras. I've also always been able to remember my life on the Other Side, as well as the experience of being born into this lifetime as Belinda.

This doesn't make me exceptional, though. Most children are born sensitive and intuitive and can still remember their homes and lives on the Other Side. What was exceptional about me, however, is that, for whatever reason, my psychic and intuitive abilities didn't fade as I grew older – they got stronger. With every passing year, I remembered more; I saw more. And I retained memories about my life *before* this life, which other children seemed to lose.

Because of this, growing up I felt like a foreigner, a stranger in this world. I learned that seeing inside people was bad, and that talking about it was even worse. I learned that it wasn't right or good to know things and see things like angels, ghosts, energy and people's thoughts and feelings; and that it was frowned upon (and punishable) to be deep-feeling and aware. This left me feeling displaced and estranged.

I didn't want to be shunned; I wanted to be loved. So as a child, I pretended to be someone else. I pretended not to see; I pretended not to know. But I couldn't help seeing what I did, and knowing what I knew.

That was until my late teens, when I discovered my gifts could help others, and that in the process, my psychic and intuitive abilities, although unusual, could actually bring me *closer* to others. I learned how to connect to others through my gifts. And when people began confiding in me, telling me they were like me but were scared to come out of the (spiritual) closet, I realised I wasn't alone. There are others who are sensitive and intuitive; others who also feel estranged here on earth. The sensitives among us are the intuitives, the empaths, the mediums, the seers and the healers. We are the ones born with feet in both worlds – the earth plane and the spiritual realms. We are the ones who often suffer because we don't know how to navigate between these worlds.

In a world where we're increasingly unsure and uncertain, we are feeling even less connected and more removed from ourselves than ever. We're losing touch with our own spiritual and physical selves, with our relationships, with our intuition, with our light. We know something isn't right – we know we need to change and heal our lives. We know we need to embrace our intuitive gifts, but we don't know how to get started. That is why I wrote this book.

I am Belinda Davidson and I've been working as a professional intuitive for more than twenty years. Discovering that I could use my gifts to help others was a turning point for me. After many years as a medical intuitive, I also began working as a spiritual coach and mentor, teaching people about chakras, intuition and all things pertaining to the spiritual and mystical path. On my website (www.belindadavidson.com) I regularly post articles and offer free spiritual support. Tens of thousands of people subscribe to my newsletter.

You can think of *Find Your Light* as a manual – a guide on how to balance and align your chakras and get in touch with your own psychic and intuitive capabilities, whatever form they take. Once you do that, you'll discover your purpose for being here at this time, and you can start to use your mystical skills to accomplish it.

Part I outlines my personal journey – my early struggles with my psychic abilities and how I came to realise that they were a gift, not a burden, and could be used to help others.

Part II introduces the twelve chakras that make up each person's energy field. I take you through each individual chakra, outlining its purpose, and what can happen if it becomes weak or blocked. I explain how these chakras work together, and introduce you to my Chakra Cleanse Meditation, which can heal your chakras and transform your life.

It's my sincerest wish that this book and the techniques in it bring you comfort, clarity and purpose.

PART 1

FROM DARK TO LIGHT

CHAPTER 1

INCARNATION

Most of us don't remember our time as infants, let alone the months spent in our mother's womb. We don't recall our first joys or our early sorrows. Most of us. But I do. I remember being in utero and being born, and I remember coming into this world filled with fear.

During my gestation, I felt the lightness of my spirit-form fade to dark as I was pulled like an anchor down to the earth plane. I remember dreading the heaviness of the world, its violence and aggression, and knowing that I would feel trapped and estranged here. And it was with this sadness that my soul began its incarnation as Belinda Davidson.

I came here carrying another ache as well – one that belonged not to me, but to my mother, who was grieving the loss of her own mother.

Nine months before, I'd been hurriedly conceived in the hope that I would meet my Grandma Jean, who was dying of cancer. She and Mum wanted the three of us to have time together before her departure. Sadly, a meeting in this place was not to be – my grandmother died five months before I was born. Instead, we bonded in another way.

In the final stages of her illness, Grandma Jean looked at my mum clutching a list of baby names and told her she only needed to consider the ones for girls. Grandma Jean was a psychic and intuitive, and as she left this life and I entered it, passing each other like shooting stars in the night, her knowing I was to be a girl, me knowing we weren't to meet in 'real time', she imprinted upon me her talents – an array of otherworldly and sensitive abilities. While Jean's gifts enabled me to carry on her legacy, they would prove difficult for a child to carry.

My arrival here was unremarkable by all external accounts. I was born in Sydney and when I was still a baby, we left the city in favour of a quieter, beachside life. My father had just graduated from medical school and, feeling professional competition in Sydney, moved us to the Central Coast.

Dad was clever and charismatic and with his movie-star looks, he was usually the centre of attention. From the moment he walked into a room, he filled it up, and although Mum had the looks and brains to rival his, his commanding personality far overshadowed hers.

A teacher, Mum had given up her career to support my father and care for our family. Pleasant and easygoing, she was the peacekeeper – a necessary role in our family because of Dad's white-hot temper, which we all learned to fear.

My parents moved us to the Central Coast to better Dad's work prospects, but also to bring us closer to his parents, Grandad George and Nanna Merle.

Grandad George was a striking man of Scottish descent. He'd immigrated to Australia with his seven brothers and sisters when he was just fourteen, but his soft, lilting accent remained. He was olive-skinned and blue-eyed, and had a deep love of philosophy and Christianity.

Some of my fondest memories of childhood were at my grandparents' house. I remember helping Grandad in his vegetable patch. While showing me how to pluck caterpillars from leaves or pat the earth down hard so the seeds didn't move, he'd tell me about his belief in hope and redemption.

'God loves you for who you are, Belinda. Do you know that?' I reach for a spinach leaf, my tiny fingers wrapping around the smooth wriggling body of an earthworm. I squint at it, then up at Grandad.

'What does that mean?' I ask.

Grandad George kneels, sets down his pick and spade, and draws the back of a gloved hand across his damp brow.

His blue eyes sparkle. His voice is gentle. 'You don't need to do anything to be deserving of God's love. You just need to let him into your heart.'

I'm unsure of how to do that – let God into my heart. All I know is that being in the garden patch with Grandad George is one of my favourite things in the world.

Nanna Merle was another story. A nervous person with a fragile temperament, she was plain and withdrawn, and rarely went outside. She could usually be found in the kitchen baking biscuits and cakes, tidying her already immaculate house, or in her bedroom having one of her 'turns'.

These occurred frequently. She'd have a fizzy drink to calm her stomach, then retire to her room and draw the blinds. Our job was to be quiet and leave her in peace. But Nanna was sweet and kind; she even smelled sweet, like she was sugar-dusted. And I loved to nestle into her, nudging and burying myself deep in her doughy arms and breasts.

Throughout my early childhood, I adored the devoted attention of Grandad George and Nanna Merle, but it was my mother's deep love that soothed me. We'd sit together on a large rug on the grass under the eucalyptus tree in our backyard, or lie on the floor in the living room. We'd play, or she would read to me. Many mornings she'd take me to the beach.

Mum plonks me down in the sand, then smiles as I start to topple over. I watch the light above her head zigzag and reflect off her big sunglasses, sending shooting sparkles into my eyes. She adjusts my chubby legs until I can sit upright, and then she sits down next to me, shielding me. She scoops sand over my legs and tickles my tummy. Her dark hair falls down around me like a soft, airy cloak, and she laughs and laughs and tickles me some more. I hear the steady crash of waves in the background as Mum's warm body presses against mine. I feel safe.

Outwardly safe, that is. Inside I was still frightened about being on earth. As a toddler, life felt narrow and restricted. I didn't like being confined to a little body that didn't move properly. It was hard not being able to express the complexities of what I was thinking and feeling. And it was all so alien to the clarity and expanse I knew as my real self.

Though challenging, in the first few years I didn't feel completely alone. In addition to the loving care of my mum and grandparents, I had a companion – one friend who understood me and kept me company: Julie.

Julie and I would be in my bedroom for hours, chatting away, playing with my dolls or doing dress-ups.

'You can be a green princess, Julie. I'll be the red princess.'
I hold out a silver crown speckled with emeralds.

Julie crosses the rainbow-striped rug and sits down beside me.

I put the crown down next to her and pick up the one with bright red rubies.

'I always wanted to be a red princess.' I smile, placing the crown on my head. 'Red princesses are beautiful.'

Julie's eyes are large and hazel. I pick up the green crown and place it on her head.

'See – you're a green princess!'

Julie laughs and we both close our eyes and travel to our secret, imagined place together where we are princesses in a castle.

Mum appears in the doorway and looks across the room. 'Are you playing with Julie?' she asks. Julie and I both nod.

Mum knew Julie as my imaginary friend. She'd buckle Julie in for the car ride or set a place for her at the table. She'd read us bedtime stories, and sometimes she'd even tuck both of us in at night.

Like most imaginary friends, Julie would appear whenever I was ready to play with her. But what Mum didn't know was that Julie never left my side because she wasn't imaginary. At night-time, or when I was happy playing alone, caught up in my own secret child-world, Julie would simply sit in the corner of my room and wait. She could sit like that – statue-like, atrophied – for hours. When I wanted to play with her, she'd sort of reanimate. Colour would flush back into her cheeks, and she'd join in my game.

Though she talked and played like other children, even back then I knew Julie was different. She was about five years old and always looked the same – barefoot, her hair dark, long and tangled, and she wore an old-fashioned lace nightgown. Julie didn't look solid; she was transparent, like a watermark. Hazy and slightly out of focus. The exception was her eyes, which were always hazel, clear and sad.

Julie never spoke aloud to me. Instead, she would send images and thoughts into my mind, and sometimes I would do the same with her. Telepathic communication had been familiar to me since before my birth, before I ever met Julie. It was how we'd 'spoken' on the Other Side, where we were all clairaudient and could read and hear each other's thoughts. It seemed normal to me that people on earth would communicate that way too.

But soon, I would learn just how abnormal I was.

Inheriting Grandma Jean's psychic gifts and remembering where I'd come from made me an unusually deep-thinking toddler. I had an insatiable need to understand everything and a peculiar sort of intelligence. I could speak fluently before I was two years old and would articulate complex concepts and theories. I was always asking questions beyond my years. Adults found this either charming or disconcerting.

When I was two years old, I waddled up to my mother wearing only a nappy and asked her how babies came into this world. Used to my deep and probing questions, she did her best to explain the complexities of human reproduction. When she was through, I paused, then posed another question.

'So, how do you stop babies from being made?'

My mother couldn't believe she'd had to give the contraceptive talk to a two-year-old! But my strangely philosophical questions weren't what unnerved adults most; it was the way I tried to counsel them about their problems.

Growing up, I spent lots of time in Dad's surgery. Mum worked as his receptionist and I loved to help her process people's payments, answer the phone and tidy and stack the magazines in the waiting room. But my attempts to help Dad weren't as welcome. Ever since I can remember, I've been able to see inside a person and discover everything about them, including what is making them unwell. Inside and around everyone is a field of light, called an *energy field*. When I look deep into a person's energy field, it shows me their chakras. And if I look deeper into each chakra, I can see tiny motion pictures of people's lives. While Dad's patients were waiting for their appointments, I would look into their energy fields

13

and chakras, watching the little movies and colours there. I could see why they'd come and I wanted to talk to them about it. I was completely unaware that other people didn't have the same ability; I thought everyone saw what I did. So when adults got angry because I told them what I saw, I was confused. They would deny what I was saying, even though I could clearly see it was true. That upset me – why were they lying?

'I'm not angry!' a young, blonde-haired woman yelled at me, even though her energy field was bright red and hot with rage.

'I'm not sad!' an elderly man shouted in my face, though I knew he cried every night over the death of his wife.

I was called many things by angry adults: rude, nosy, 'too big for my boots'. I quickly learned to stop telling them what I saw.

I knew it wasn't their fault. They didn't remember their connection to the Other Side – that beautiful place of peace and light where we are all unconditionally loved and connected to each other – and that meant they both hurt inside and were hurtful to others. They were selfish and defensive because they'd forgotten where they came from. But their reactions made me feel homesick.

It hurt to think about the Other Side, about how much I missed it and how far away it was. About how loving and light and clear everything was over there, and how foggy and dark and angry everything was here.

My little heart had a gaping hole and I had no idea how to fill it.

CHAPTER 2

VISITORS

As life went on, I got used to being in a body again. I could control it more easily and started to feel less burdened about being a child. I still needed to hide parts of myself – I knew it wasn't safe to talk to adults about what I saw within them or how they were feeling – but I no longer felt quite so confined. Julie continued to be my best friend and playmate, and after my sister Tanya was born in 1981, I came to rely on Julie's friendship more than ever. Tanya's arrival turned my two-and-a-half-year-old world upside down.

When Mum brought Tanya home from the hospital, I blocked the entrance way, screaming, 'You're not going to bring that thing into this house! Nooooo!' Whether it was psychic knowledge or simply a toddler's natural reaction, my hunch about my sister was right. Tanya was a distressed baby.

She cried almost constantly and slept and fed poorly. Because of this, all Mum's attention was now focused on Tanya, and it seemed like I'd lost the only human friend I'd had. Julie became the only one I felt connected to.

I'm unaware of having seen or communicated with other ghosts before Julie. She was an earthbound spirit – a spirit trapped on earth – so she was sad and lost. But she wasn't mean or unkind – on the contrary! Julie was fun and gentle. But I quickly came to learn that this was not typical behaviour for ghosts.

When I was around four years old, ghosts started visiting me at night. As soon as Mum tucked me in and turned out the light, they would come into my room, sliding up underneath my bedroom door or materialising through the walls. Some would plop down from the ceiling like fat spiders. They looked like people, with bodies and faces that resembled those of men and women, but they also looked shadowy and, like Julie, they were transparent and 'blurred' looking. From a few feet away they were just dark moving shapes. Up close, they were terrifying.

A ghost still has the same physical attributes they did when they were alive – the same gender, body shape, hair and eye colour, and so on. But their ghost form becomes imprinted with the negative emotions that prevented them from transitioning to the Other Side. The feelings the person couldn't release drench their earthbound form, making them look like a tainted, gnarled version of their old self.

If I didn't close my eyes before they reached my bed, I would see in horrific detail the remnants of their negative emotions. Ghosts who were trapped in bitterness and resentment had long, skeletal faces that dripped like wax. Those who were full of rage or hate had large, engorged faces with flaming eyes and shark-like teeth. Jealous or envious ghosts had sullen and sunken faces and forms, and depressed ghosts had twisted faces and hunched bodies.

But it was the sad ghosts I feared the most, with their swollen and tear-stained faces. They weren't as menacing as the others, but they were much more frightening because they would reach out and touch me.

Their slimy, tentacle-like hands would slip in under my duvet and poke around my ankles and legs. Then, as more and more sad ghosts arrived, jostling for position, they would start to grab at me. Soon, their hands would be all over my body, and though I'd move and thrash about, their grip was so strong I couldn't shake them loose.

Some nights, ghosts would chase me through the house. I began to dread night-time.

My eyes are shut tight. I breathe deep, thinking maybe I can ignore it. Maybe I can get back to sleep. But it's no use – my bladder is practically bursting. I have to go to the bathroom!

I wonder if he's still there. Slowly, I open my eyes. From the corner of the room the old ghost man smiles at me, licking his scaly lips in anticipation. He's just sitting there, waiting for his opportunity to pounce.

I hold my breath and move slowly, placing a tentative foot on the floor. He hunches forward, his grin widening.

I suddenly remember that Mum had left a cup of water for me, which I'd drunk before bed. I snatch the empty cup from my nightstand and shove it under the covers and start to pee, my eyes fixed on the ghost. His grin fades and he slouches back into the seat, eyes downturned. There will be no fun for him tonight.

I didn't turn to my parents for help with the ghosts. Like many parents whose children claim to see ghosts, mine thought it was 'all in my head'. Just a child's overactive imagination.

On the odd occasion when I did crawl out of bed and run down the hall to Mum and Dad, I was always sent back to bed and told to stop being silly. And by running to their room, I risked having a ghost chase me down the hallway. So there didn't seem to be any point in asking for their help. Even if they did believe me, they wouldn't have been able to understand what was happening.

My parents weren't alone – the truth is, most of us don't understand the nature of ghosts. We don't understand what ghosts are or how they become stuck here.

When a person is unable to find the light after death and can't leave their connection to the earth plane and move on into the Other Side, they remain bound to earth. This can happen if the natural flow of passing from earth (leaving their human body) and returning to their spirit body on the Other Side is interrupted in some way, and there are many ways this can occur.

Some people can't transition into the light after death because they are religious and fear the wrath of God – they fear they haven't been 'good' in life and won't get into heaven. Others harbour secrets, guilt, shame or anger, and can't release these emotions and move on. Some people, even after they've died and left their human body behind, feel angry and resentful because they feel they were taken before their time. Others simply don't know they're dead because nobody is there to help them move over.

When we die, most of us find the light. We receive help from our deceased loved ones and angels, and we can easily make the transition from our earthly life to our spirit life. Most of us. But some of us, sadly, stay earthbound.

I was born a ghost whisperer. I was born able to see and communicate with earthbound spirits. My psychic and empathic abilities made me a beacon to ghosts, and so they flocked to me.

But I didn't know any of this when I was a child. I didn't know they were trapped, troubled and lonely. I was scared of ghosts the way children are scared of monsters and bogeymen and shadows. Scary dead people came to me when Mum turned out the light, and these scary dead people did scary things to me. All I knew is that I was petrified of night-time. All I knew is that I was petrified of what I could see.

If I had known back then that I was a ghost whisperer and that I could protect myself from ghosts, as well as help them find the light, I wouldn't have lived in terror.

But it would be many more years before I'd learn this.

CHAPTER 3

EXORCISM

In 1988, when I was ten years old, my family – which by then also included my baby brother, Aaron – moved to the Gold Coast. One day, while we were still living on the Central Coast, Dad, bored with the sermon in the Salvation Army church, took a stroll and found himself at a Pentecostal church. He was so taken by the vibrancy and modernity of the church that he decided, then and there, that it would be our new spiritual home. Within a few months, Dad found a new job and we relocated to be a part of a Pentecostal church that was starting on the Gold Coast.

I hated our new rental house the moment I set foot inside it. It was a large, looming, two-storey dark-brick house that smelled of mould and shadow secrets. Inside were cheap plastic fittings, ugly, orange-brown coloured carpet and curtains, and nails and wood poking out from the floor and walls. It was oddly built, with each room completely boxed off from the others, so when you were by yourself it felt as if you were in a tomb.

While the inside of the house was shadowy, the outside was scorching. The brick walls, verandah and play area both reflected and absorbed the sun, so when we played outside, we'd burn our eyes and bodies. We hated outside playtime, along with the garden and its freaky inhabitants.

It was in this garden that we first saw a cane toad. We were petrified of the huge amphibians with their bulging eyes and poisonous saliva. They were everywhere, hopping around or just sitting there like fat, warty-looking lumps. There were other nasty things in the garden: huge wasps with long stinging tails; big jumping ants that would scurry up our legs and bite us all over; and patches of prickles that would sting our feet and wedge themselves between our toes. But while the outside of the house was downright hostile, it was the inside that terrified us.

Inside, it always felt like we were being followed. Tanya and Aaron didn't share my abilities, but they could feel it too. Wherever we went – upstairs to our room, to the bathroom, to the garage to get ice cream from the freezer – it was as if some-thing was after us . . . This was confirmed when that something started grabbing our shoulders and jumping onto our backs.

Tanya, Aaron and I started to move as a group, travel-ling together everywhere we went inside the house. After watching us do this for a few weeks, Mum asked what we were doing. When we told her something was following us, and that it sometimes chased us too, Mum was understandably concerned.

The presence would also come near us when we were going to sleep at night. Tanya and I shared a room, and when the lights went out she'd jump up onto my top bunk and we'd sleep pressed tightly together. Aaron would often run in from his room and sleep in Tanya's empty bottom bunk. This didn't stop us from seeing dark shapes moving across the room or menacing faces peering down at us, but at least we weren't alone.

Although I was scared of 'the something' (along with all the other scary things that showed up at night), I was also relieved. I was no longer alone in my terror; no longer the only one seeing ghosts.

But this relief was short-lived. I was about to have one of the most terrifying experiences of all.

I'm sitting on the front step waiting for the pastor to arrive. It's hot outside and I'm shielding my eyes against the sun, watching the street for his car.

Mum told me that the pastor is going to help us. He's going to pray over me and it will break the curse that's on our family, the one responsible for the ghosts in the house. Mum says it's because her father was a Freemason; that's why we're cursed. That's why I'm cursed. And since I'm the firstborn, if the pastor prays over me, the curse will be broken.

I don't understand what Mum means. I don't know what curses or Freemasons are, but I understand there is something 'over' me and Tanya and Aaron, something around and inside us that's wrong.

'He'll just pray over you,' Mum says, seeing my apprehension, 'that's all. It won't take long.'

When the pastor arrives, Mum scurries out of the kitchen, patting her hair and giving the house a final once-over. She and the pastor exchange a few hurried words, then he motions for me to follow him down the hall. He's flushed and dressed as if he's on his way to preach at church. When we reach the living room, he points to a white towel Mum has laid out over the orange carpet on the floor. He tells me to lie down. The white towel looks tiny on the sea of orange carpet. My stomach lurches and I want to run away, but I don't want to make the pastor mad. Once, when I was at his house for a playdate with his daughter, he hit me across the face. No one else was around to see it, and when Mum asked him about it later, he said I'd made it up. He said I was a liar.

He's one of those adults who pretends to like children, but really doesn't. His energy field goes red and mean around kids. I am scared of being prayed over, but I'm more scared of being hit again.

'Close your eyes now,' the pastor says, 'and don't open them until I tell you that you can.'

I shut my eyes.

'And lie still. Don't move at all.'

I lie as still as I can, with my eyes shut tight. My heart is thumping. My legs feel loose and trembly.

Then the pastor begins to pray. His voice is clear and loud above me.

'Dear Jesus, dear almighty Lord and Saviour, may thy will be done today in the name of Jesus. Today we come before you to ask you to release this child from the curse placed upon her; the curse that her grandfather placed over his grandchildren when he was involved in the Freemasonry church. This child has been cursed – enslaved and ensnared by Lucifer, by Satan, the Devil, the king of deceit and lies and darkness. We ask today, dear Jesus, dear Lord and our Saviour, that this curse be broken and this child be freed from darkness.'

I'm trying to lie still and keep my eyes closed, but my heart is pumping fast. I want to run away.

'This child needs to be freed from the Devil and the demons that are within her. I call upon the blood of Christ to break this curse and free her!'

The pastor places his palm on my forehead and I flinch. His hand is red hot and prickly.

'I pray in God's name that this child, now, be freed from the curse! From the Devil and the demons! I rebuke the Devil! I rebuke the darkness! I rebuke the demons, those vile spirits of darkness that have attached themselves to the child. Demons – I rebuke you!'

Suddenly, a wave of heat rushes from my feet up to my head. First, it feels like warm water, but then it becomes so hot it's nearly boiling. White-hot rays of pain flash through me.

'Come forth demons, I say! Leave the body of this child!'

The pain is growing stronger, collecting in my chest and throat. It's pain like I've never experienced. I'm on fire! I'm boiling up!

'In the name of Jesus Christ, our Saviour and Lord,' yells the pastor, 'I command that the demons now come forth! Come forth demons and leave the body of this child!'

The pain is unbearable. I'm choking on it and spluttering; still trying to lie still, still trying to obey.

'In the Name of Jesus, I COMMAND the demons: Leave the body of this child!!!'

I can no longer lie still. I begin to scream.

The pastor starts to talk in a fast, babbling language that makes no sense. The adults in the church call this 'speaking in tongues'. God's gibberish. I don't know what he's saying. All I know is that I'm being boiled alive, and that something is trying to push its way out of my throat.

Waves of terror crash over me. The energy that's being pulled out of me is fighting to stay in. It's scratching and scraping and trying to hold on to my legs and abdomen. I'm being ripped apart. I can't stop screaming because it's coming out through my mouth!

I'm screaming in complete terror, not only because of the pain, but because, suddenly, I understand what's happening: Evil is inside me and it's coming out!

I wake up exhausted. My throat's sore, my body is drenched in sweat and the room is spinning. I must have passed out. Before the full weight of the realisation can sink in – that I am bad and evil and was possessed by demons – Grandma Jean appears. She materialises above me, then moves to sit next to me. I recognise her from the photos Mum has *showed me. Her eyes are dark and kind, and she takes my hand in hers.*

'Belinda' – she looks me deep in my eyes – 'right now, people don't understand you or your gifts, but when you grow up this will change. One day, many people will want to know what you see and hear. They will love you for it. And they will uphold you for it. Not hurt you for it, like they are now.'

She squeezes my hand, but I'm too dizzy and shocked to feel comforted.

'Ignore this silly man,' she says, gesturing to the pastor, who is still kneeling next to me and babbling in tongues, 'for they know not what they do.'

And with that, just as suddenly as she appeared, she leaves.

I open my eyes again. The pastor is gone. I'm alone in the room and it's quiet.

I stand up, unsteady, weak and sore, and walk out of the room. I glance back briefly at the tiny white towel on the mass of orange carpet. Then I go up to my bedroom and shut the door.

Grandma Jean was right, of course – I wasn't possessed. I didn't have demons in me. And there wasn't any curse on my family.

When we moved into the rental house, unbeknown to us, we'd moved into a haunted house. It had such bad energy that it attracted dark spirits. Years later, we found out that someone had been murdered there before we moved in. (And years after that, we heard that someone was murdered there after we moved out.)

The pastor, in his Pentecostal fervour and naiveté, sincerely believed we were cursed and thought he could help us. But his version of help was misguided and harmful . . . During that exorcism my soul was torn out of my body. It wasn't demons clinging to me, fighting to stay inside me. It was my soul!

The physical and emotional trauma of having my soul cast out of my body created a huge tear in my energy field, severely disabling me. It was akin to puncturing a lung or being run over by a car – something one can barely survive.

My soul wasn't completely severed from my body that day. If it had been, I would have died. But the damage to my energy field was enormous; it removed any psychic protection I'd had. Being born psychic had already made me sensitive and vulnerable. But after the exorcism, I was psychically crippled. I had no protection against people's illnesses or their negative thoughts and feelings and, as a result, I became very unwell. Before the exorcism, I would receive instant impressions about people's feelings and pain, but once I moved away from the person those impressions mostly disappeared. After the exorcism, however, I had no filter. Once I received an impression about someone, I couldn't stop feeling how they felt. Their pain and anguish, both physical and mental, began to lodge itself in my energy field – I *absorbed* it.

Usually this happened in my father's surgery. When I'd look into a person's energy field – even for the briefest moment – their sickness and life problems would jump out of their energy field and into mine.

Sometimes I knew their problems had 'come into me' and that they were making me feel unwell. But many times – because it happened instantaneously – I didn't know what was taking place. I would suddenly feel these strange, strong pains in my body and not know why.

The pains were bizarre and irregular. I'd experience heaviness in my chest and torso (it felt like a large person sitting on me); deep cold pains in my back, legs and feet (like being pricked by ice needles); strange sensations of burning and pressure in my head and violent stomach cramps that would leave me curled over and retching. These pains would hit me suddenly, then leave just as quickly as they came.

These sensations were my body's way of trying to process the huge amounts of negativity being dumped into my energy field each and every day. I was experiencing *empath syndrome* – a very real condition that happens to sensitive, intuitive and deeply feeling people if they don't learn to 'clear' and protect their energy field. Of course, Dad didn't know this. He ran tests and asked his fellow doctors for help, but they couldn't find an explanation for my pain. I was diagnosed with hypochondria and told that it was 'all in my head'. So I stopped telling Mum and Dad what I was feeling.

As terrible as these physical sensations were, becoming someone else was absolute agony. As well as experiencing pain because I was trying to filter out people's negativity, I was also suffering because I was absorbing other people's traumas.

One afternoon I sat next to one of Dad's patients in his surgery – a kind, elderly woman. She had been raped by her father when she was a teenager, and the trauma of this rape was still in her energy field. Because she had never told anyone about what had happened, the pain lay there, large and wounded, inside her. It was causing the constant stomach and blood pressure problems she was having. She didn't know this, but I did, because I could see it in her energy field and chakras. As we talked about school and whether I liked my grade-four teacher, her pain leapt into me. And that night, I *experienced* her rape.

Once, I vomited for hours after I sat next to a woman on a bus who was undergoing chemotherapy. On another occasion, I spent three days wanting to kill myself.

'Belinda, are you awake?' Natalie asks as she walks into my room.

She knows I'm awake, because I always wait up for her to come upstairs and say 'hi'. She's here every Thursday night for the Bible study group Mum and Dad run for teens from our church.

Natalie's one of those nice teenagers who talks to you like you're her peer. I often sit next to her in church. I love listening to her high, clear voice as she sings the psalms.

She's usually sweet and asks me how I am, or how school's going. But tonight she just walks over to my bed and sits down, and I see that her eyes are teary and swollen.

'Are you okay?' I ask.

'Oh, I don't know,' she says, swallowing hard. 'Something strange is happening to me. I feel depressed.'

I don't know what the word 'depressed' means, but I can sense how she feels. She's heavy and sad. All of a sudden

I can hear the mean voices in her head. They're saying horrible things to her.

'I don't like myself very much,' she says. 'I don't think I'm going to make it.'

I open my mouth to respond, but a voice calls up from downstairs saying youth group is starting. Natalie jumps off the bed and rushes out of the room.

Even though Natalie's gone, her depression is still here. It's clinging to me, and I feel heavy and sick.

For the next few days, I had a torrent of angry, vicious voices in my head. 'You're worthless!' they screamed. 'You're an idiot! You're fat, lazy and disgusting! You'll never amount to anything!'

For three whole days I was bombarded by these savage, cruel thoughts. I had picked up Natalie's self-hate and was under attack.

On Sunday when I saw Natalie at church, I told her I knew how she was feeling. 'There are voices in your head saying mean things to you, like you're worthless and fat and lazy, and this is making you feel bad. But these voices are those of your father,' I said. I knew this intuitively. 'You hate yourself. You keep thinking about how much you hate yourself.'

Tears began to slide down her cheeks. 'Nobody knows this about me. Nobody except you. You won't tell anyone, will you, Belinda? I'm scared other people will find out and think I'm crazy.' I assured her I wouldn't tell anyone, then I sat with her until she finished crying. I never heard those voices after that, but the experience was frightening.

I didn't know then that the ability to see the dark in others is a gift. I didn't know I had been born an empath, and that I had the ability to see people's shadows and help them heal their fears and negativity.

It wasn't until much later in my life, many years after I started working as a medical intuitive, that I would discover this about myself. There would be many more years of struggle with my own shadow, and those of others, before my path would reveal itself.

CHAPTER 4

TRUTH-TELLING

As I moved into puberty, my psychic sensitivities seemed to intensify. What I didn't know then is that it's quite common for psychics, intuitives and empaths to experience an increase in intensity during the teen years. Hormonal changes can bring about a spike in our extrasensory abilities.

I was still struggling with the after-effects of the exorcism at this time, including digestive and other health problems. I felt exhausted, stressed and depressed. And now, on top of that, I had to cope with even stronger psychic abilities. The shadows inside people suddenly looked even larger and more menacing.

I was also struggling to figure out what I could tell people about what I saw without getting into trouble. In my first year of high school I was sent out of class because of something

I psychically knew. My home economics teacher, Mrs Dawson, had been absent for several weeks. As soon as she walked into the room, I knew why – she was pregnant.

When I saw Mrs Dawson, a strong pang of nausea leapt out of her body and into mine. The sickness landed smack bang in my solar plexus and I thought I was going to vomit. When I looked inside her energy field, I saw a tiny baby growing in her tummy.

When Mum was pregnant with my younger sister Rebekah, she'd been sick in bed in the mornings. I knew that having a tiny baby inside you could make you sick, and I knew this was called morning sickness.

I felt sorry for my teacher. She had really bad morning sickness, but her husband had made her go back to work so they would have more money. I liked her a lot too; she was pretty and kind. So I asked her, 'Have you recovered from morning sickness now?'

Mrs Dawson froze, her pretty face turning white with shock. She stared at me, blinking and swallowing, then pointed a long, shaky finger at me and said in a low voice, 'You are a gossip and a liar, Belinda Davidson, and you aren't to be trusted.'

She sent me out of the classroom. I spent the morning crouched and crying against a brick wall next to the home economics room. I still felt nauseous, just like she did, and I also felt sad and confused. I really liked Mrs Dawson, but she didn't like me anymore.

There were many other incidents like that during my teen years.

Dad's friend, Donald, is at our house for dinner. I don't like him much — he's one of those adults who speaks down to children, always lecturing and sermonising. But he loves to tell stories. He boasts about his new cars or motorcycles, or his latest heroic and chivalrous deeds. He speaks with his mouth full, and it's fun to watch the way food and spittle fly through the air and land in chunks all around him.

Tonight, though, Donald isn't his usual self. He's subdued and quiet, picking at his food and moving it around his plate.

I sigh and pick at my food too. I was really looking forward to being entertained. Why isn't he his usual self tonight? Maybe if I look inside his energy field, I can see what's wrong?

I look into Donald and see he's thinking about a dark-haired woman. She is petite and has curvy hips and a pert bottom. He plans to visit her after dinner, and he's wishing he could leave now to go and be with her. He's feeling uneasy about it. I can see that he's kissed and had sex with her like married people do.

I'm confused. In Sunday school they tell us we're only supposed to kiss and love the person we are married to. But this woman isn't Donald's wife; Donald's wife is tall and blonde and loves to laugh. Why is he loving someone else?

So I ask him, 'Who is the woman with the brown hair that you're going to visit after dinner?'

Donald's head spins towards me like he's heard a gunshot. He's staring at me with his mouth hanging open.

'Wh-, wh-, what did you say?' he asks, his voice croaky and shaky.

I know that when adults are shocked by something, they get angry. And when adults get angry, they usually hurt kids. I don't want to repeat my question. I shrink down in my seat, wishing I could disappear.

'What did you say?' he asks again, speaking slowly, looking me straight in the eyes.

I stay quiet.

'I said, what did you say?' His voice is louder now, and menacing.

Finally, I say softly, while keeping my eyes fixed on the table, 'Who is the woman with the brown hair you're going to see after dinner?'

For a moment it's quiet. Then he leans across the table and, sticking his big face into mine, his eyes bulging and wild, yells, 'You should mind your own business, you creepy kid!'

Donald snatches his keys and wallet and storms out.

No one at the table says anything. I'm relieved Dad isn't home from work, otherwise he'd yell at me too.

I climb down from my chair and go off to play alone in my room.

These incidents were confusing and scary, but that wasn't the only thing making my life difficult. Even more ghosts were appearing in my room at bedtime, and they would often stay all night long.

Before, after fighting them off for a while, I could eventually fall asleep. But now their pursuit of me was relentless.

The combined effects of the exorcism and puberty had left me extremely vulnerable.

Night after night I thrashed around, fighting off the ghosts. Finally I would fall asleep, only to be jolted awake again by a ghost grabbing my ankle or stroking my hair.

Thus began a chronic pattern of night terrors and insomnia that would take many years to overcome. In the meantime, I developed a coping mechanism. I became two people: *Daytime Belinda* and *Night-time Belinda*.

Daytime Belinda was the girl who woke up in the morning, brushed her teeth, went off to school and had no knowledge of what was happening to Night-time Belinda. Daytime Belinda knew she was unusual; she knew she could see inside people and discover things about them that she wasn't supposed to know, but she had no clue about what took place when the lights went out. That was Night-time Belinda's problem. Daytime Belinda began as soon as I woke up in the morning. With the fresh light of day, Night-time Belinda was erased, and Daytime Belinda would greet the dawn.

Many experts in child psychology say that this type of dissociation is a common way that children cope with trauma – they erase certain things from their consciousness so they can survive. They also say this occurs more often in cases where children don't get help, or don't feel safe talking about what's happening to them.

I had to deal with it all alone. So I lived this way, split into Daytime and Night-time Belinda, for many years.

CHAPTER 5

ANGELS

When I was a child, I didn't know about the Law of Resonance – *that like energy attracts like energy*. I didn't understand that all the fear I brought into this world had caused dark and scary spiritual things to happen to me. My fear created fear.

As my psychic, intuitive, empath, ghost-whispering and truth-telling nature and abilities blossomed, and I was rebuked, silenced and punished, my fear grew. My life had become layers of things I was deeply afraid of – things about myself.

By the time I was a teenager, I wanted to leave this terrible life on earth behind. I wanted to return to the light-filled, joy-filled expanse and delight of my soul-self on the Other Side.

I began to dream about my own death. And some months later, it almost happened.

The big white church bus comes to a stop in the parking lot. It's practically bouncing as the teens inside buzz with excitement. One of the best things about being fourteen is that I finally get to be part of the youth group. We're spending today at the water park.

The door of the bus opens and we all run off towards the wave pool.

'Let's go far out back and catch the biggest waves!' someone yells.

I stand there looking at the huge pool with its crashing waves, and I hesitate. I'm not a strong swimmer and I don't like going in the ocean when it's rough. But the other kids are already jumping in, and I don't want to miss out. I follow them.

Right away the waves come so fast and hard I can't manage to get over them in time. I drop beneath the surface, trying to duck them, but I'm not fast enough. I start to panic.

A huge wave crashes over me and I'm pulled under. I struggle to the surface and open my mouth to gasp for air, but another wave is already crashing down on me. My mouth fills with water as I'm pushed down again. I'm fighting to find the surface, choking, kicking and thrashing about, but I can't tell which way is up. My body is flipping over and over. Everything's spinning.

Then everything starts to slow. I'm floating near the bottom of the pool and all around me are legs and bodies — hundreds of adults and children at play, and everyone is moving in slow motion. Skinny boys' legs kicking and jumping; strong men's legs, muscled and pumping power-fully; soft women's legs moving and swimming; chubby babies with their legs kicking like little pistons. All of it happening as if time is merely inching itself forward . . .

Then I feel my body moving. A current pulls me to the right, then pushes me upwards to the edge of the pool. I realise I'm nearing the surface, so I make a grab for the wall. But the tiles are slippery and my fingers keep sliding off.

I keep trying, fighting to pull myself up, but I keep slipping back down. Fighting, grabbing, slipping back . . .

By now, my strength is fading; my legs are sore and limp, my lungs and throat are bursting – I'm exhausted and panicked. I feel a sort of inky black terror begin to descend . . .

I surrender. I'm underwater, near the bottom of the pool. There are those legs again, moving around me in slow, blurry motion. All those happy legs. None of them have any idea I'm drowning.

'This is it,' I think, strangely calm. 'It is now that I die.' There's a feeling of numbness and one of almost relief, that I've understood and surrendered to the inevitable.

Suddenly I find myself being lifted from the pool. Not dragged or pulled out, but lifted. I am placed, standing, on the side of the wave pool, facing away from the water.

It's as if nothing has happened. There's no water in my lungs. I'm not even panicked anymore. It's like I was never in the wave pool in the first place. There was no drowning, there was no struggle.

There's a small boy in front of me, maybe five years old.
His hair is dark brown and he's wearing black bathers.

'Are you okay?' he asks, squinting up at me.

'Yes,' I say, taking a few breaths. 'Did you pull me out
of the water?'

'Yes,' he says.

I'm about to ask him how — he's tiny — but suddenly
he's running away. He disappears into a crowd of people,
his black bathers a dark flash across a shimmering horizon.

I can't explain how, but I know my life was spared that day.
Even back then, I knew something miraculous had taken
place.

I believe an angel saved me. Either an angel gave that small
boy superhuman strength so he could pull me out of the pool,
or an angel disguised itself as a small boy to save my life. Either
way, something otherworldly had taken place which inter-
vened and kept me alive. Back then I didn't know much about
angels — they weren't something the Pentecostal church spoke
about. But somehow I knew an angel had just saved me. And
that meant there must be a purpose to my life.

Lying in bed that night, I looked at the ceiling and thanked
whoever it was that had saved my life. I didn't know if it was
God, or the angels, or some other higher power. I didn't know
what my future held or what my purpose was, but I knew
that Grandma Jean had told me the truth: that it would all be
okay in the end.

Feeling peaceful for the first time ever, for once not fearing
the ghosts or the night-time, I heard someone speak to me.

In a quiet, loving voice – a voice very different to that of people or ghosts – it said, 'The one who fears deeply can love deeply. This is your purpose. This is what you chose.'

And with that, my heart and soul at peace, I fell asleep.

CHAPTER 6

INTEGRATION

In 1993, a few weeks after my miraculous experience at the pool, my family left the Gold Coast. We moved back to the Central Coast, which was a homecoming in more ways than one; we were able to move back into our old house.

It was also a move back to Grandad George and Nanna Merle. I was so glad to be near them again. Their house had always been a refuge for me, and when we returned to the Central Coast, I started spending several nights a week there. Strangely, I don't remember ever seeing ghosts in Grandad George and Nanna Merle's home. They were so kind and caring that I sometimes wonder if their loving energy protected the entire house.

I felt safer being close to my grandparents again, and also because we had left the Pentecostal church behind. Its fanatical nature and extreme beliefs had become too much for us; all that talk of demons and curses and 'fighting against the dark' in the name of Jesus was so full of fear and negativity. After that, Mum and Dad didn't want us going to church at all, so returning to the Central Coast meant we also stopped being Christians. Having questioned the Christian faith and its teachings since I was very young, I was relieved.

In many ways, normalcy returned to our lives. I don't know why, but for a time the weird psychic stuff didn't happen as much. I began to think I'd left my dark past behind.

But you can't let go of your past if you don't heal it – if you don't accept, integrate and move beyond it – and it would take years before I could truly do that.

At the time, though, I felt that the move was a chance at a fresh start. The dark grey clouds were blowing away from my sky. In the afternoons, when I was doing my homework or writing short stories or reading a novel, the breeze off the ocean would find its way into our backyard and up into my bedroom window, its sweet salt and coolness giving me hope for a new life.

Still, it was difficult to adjust to this new life. For years, I'd had only minimal contact with people who weren't involved in the church. We'd attended Pentecostal church twice each Sunday and we'd socialised only with people from church. Because I attended a Pentecostal school, most of my friends and peers had also been Pentecostal, and we shared the same views. We all understood why it was important to talk in tongues, and why we needed to be saved and to save others before the end of the world came.

Trying to make friends with 'normal teenagers' and their 'normal issues' was challenging. I was a fish out of water, and for all of the ninth grade I was lonely.

Much of my loneliness was also because I was hiding. I was working hard to make sure my new peers didn't discover the truth about me, about my abilities or my Pentecostal past. I was scared it would somehow slip out and I'd be ostracised. I wanted to be normal. I wanted to make friends. For a while, it seemed to work. I pretended I was someone else, and they didn't seem to suspect anything.

Slowly, slowly, I began to be accepted within certain circles and started to make friends. Then, when people found out I was smoking weed, I quickly gained more friends.

Our neighbourhood was a small, seaside community. There, marijuana was easy to come by. All my neighbours and most of the kids on my street smoked weed, and grew it too. For many people, rolling a joint or smoking a few bongs was like having a beer. No big deal. I had a friend who lived in a similar neighbourhood to mine, and we'd light up in her basement.

But some of my friends at the grammar school I attended hadn't smoked weed yet. They didn't have the same access or exposure that I did.

I didn't start smoking marijuana to be popular, though. I did it because I was curious, and I loved the way it made me feel. Weed seemed to make my brain slower in a lovely, fuzzy kind of way; it made me chilled and relaxed. I was never a serious marijuana smoker, but smoking before bed helped me sleep. It would lull me into a deep rest and would stop me from experiencing (or remembering) my ghostly night-time visitations. It seemed to take the edge off my psychic sensitivities.

Weed was great, but things came to a crashing halt when, at sixteen, I tried LSD. I'd overheard one of my girlfriends talking about it at lunch. She said acid was just like weed, only much better because it made the world sparkly and cosmic. I had *no* idea it was a hard drug. My friend said she could get me some and she'd drop it off at my place. My friend Susie and I decided to try it on the weekend.

It's Saturday night and Susie and I are sitting on my bed. I can hear the faint sound of the TV from the front of the house, where my family are eating dinner.

Susie and I are looking at my hand. I'm holding two tiny pieces of something that looks like thin cardboard. They have Bart Simpson's face on them. He's smiling up at us, as if cheering us on.

We were told to take only half a tab each. I tear one in half and stick a piece under my tongue. It doesn't just look like cardboard, it tastes like it too. Susie does the same.

We wait . . . And wait . . . Nothing's happening. Where are the sparkles and cosmic visions? Maybe it's not working.

We decide to take the other half too. Still nothing's happening.

And then . . .

Suddenly I'm in a parallel universe. The world's a kaleidoscope of shifting, shimmering colours. There's the sparkly, cosmic experience we were promised!

Susie and I are sitting opposite one another, peering into each other's eyes. It's like a slideshow; I see different people inhabiting Susie and expressing themselves through her. Her face is transforming into the faces of my friends and family. What a trip!

We spend hours exploring this magical new world. A spider in the corner spins a web that grows large and turns purple. There's a fireworks display on my wall that explodes into millions of iridescent colours. Susie and I make up a private language that only we can understand, and we marvel at all the secrets the universe is revealing to us. We understand the reason for our existence and for the existence of all life forms on earth.

But something's shifting. The sparkle's fading and my visions are changing. They're becoming dark and scary – visions of blood and demons and violence.

They're getting worse and worse. I can't make them stop!

I was experiencing a psychic bleed-through. All the terrors that Night-time Belinda had experienced began to seep into the consciousness of Daytime Belinda. Visions of demons, possessions, psychic rape and violence began to rise up and pervade my psyche, like blood spreading out on a white handkerchief. I had no idea what was happening; I was completely unprepared for this purging. Pandora's box had been opened and the full weight of my traumas came bearing down on me.

While psychedelic and hallucinogenic drugs have long been used to help people confront their 'inner demons', for me it was too much, too fast. Under the right circumstances, taking drugs can be mind-opening. It's why people took LSD in the sixties, and why people go into ceremony and take ayahuasca. When used carefully and with proper support, these drugs can be life-altering and provide a spiritual and liberating experience; they can show you what needs to be healed and help you to heal it.

But I had never healed from the exorcism, and I still carried multitudes of suppressed traumas. Though I thought things were finally improving, my darkness was just lingering below the surface. The acid trip broke through that barrier, and all the trauma came rushing back into my conscious awareness. It was too much for me to handle.

After that experience, I was plagued by disturbing images. At random times during the day or night, I'd suddenly see a flash of a girl lying on the carpet with demons coming out of her mouth or a skeletal face peering over me, or I'd feel a ghost grabbing me by the throat and trying to choke me.

The image that came to me most often, and the one that scared me the most, was that of a young red-haired girl, bound and chained. She'd be falling towards me, down from the sky, reaching out to me with her bruised, bound hands. She'd be speaking to me, trying to tell me something, but her words were garbled and I couldn't understand her.

There were thousands of such pieces of myself scattered within me, floating in the abyss of my subconscious mind, wanting to weave themselves back together. I didn't know I needed to retrieve these long-lost parts of my soul so I could heal. What happened instead was that I developed panic disorder.

Although I never did acid again – and after this incident I rarely smoked weed, either – the visions and the panic I experienced after that night became even more acute. From out of nowhere I'd be hit by one of those frightening images, which would quickly bring on an anxiety attack.

Sometimes this would escalate into a full-blown panic attack, and I'd be left fighting for breath – and my life. At times I hyperventilated so badly that I would turn pink and blue. I'd dig my fingernails into my hands, making them bleed. Sometimes I'd black out.

Mum sent me to a therapist, but it didn't help. I didn't tell the therapist about the visions that were triggering the panic attacks because I was scared she'd send me to a mental hospital. I was so afraid of being institutionalised that I pretended I was scared of other things instead. I made up stories about how I was struggling at school and with my friends. For better or worse, my therapist seemed to believe me. On the one hand, I wasn't going to be institutionalised. But on the other, the therapy did nothing to resolve what was really going on.

In addition to the panic attacks, I was still experiencing other people's pain and suffering. I had grown accustomed to my empath nature; by now I was used to constantly feeling someone else's pain or malady. But after taking acid, I began to experience much more sickness. I'd spend hours in the bathroom with severe stomach pains and cramps. Sometimes my blood sugar levels would suddenly drop and I'd faint.

Dad couldn't find a cause for my low blood pressure or my stomach ailments, so once again I was diagnosed as a hypochondriac. Once again I began to hide my pain and discomfort because I didn't want Dad's disapproval, or to be seen as his 'weakling' daughter. And I still feared being labelled crazy and institutionalised.

Maybe people didn't think of me as crazy, but anyone who knew me back then would have known I was troubled. I wasn't behaviourally out of control. I wasn't in trouble with the police or addicted to drugs; I was always too cautious and sensible for that. But I was emotionally troubled; pensive, melancholic, depressive. I hated my body and face. When I looked at myself in the mirror I saw evil staring back at me.

Once again, everything seemed desperate and dark. The radiant love and beauty I'd experienced after nearly drowning at the water park was a fading memory, and I had no idea how to find my way back.

CHAPTER 7

THE TOP HOUSE

When I was seventeen Nanna Merle was diagnosed with Alzheimer's and Grandad George had a stroke. It was decided that my grandparents would move in with us so Mum could care for them. That meant some changes to our living situation.

Our house had a 'top house' – an older, smaller house in front of it that was already on the property when we bought it. It used to be Dad's surgery before he moved his practice down the street. When Grandad George and Nanna Merle moved into the main house, Tanya and I were asked to move to the top house.

At first we were thrilled. We'd have our own house and could do what we liked. We envisioned staying up all night, sleeping all day, having massive parties and getting up to all sorts of teenage shenanigans.

But right away, it was clear something was wrong. The first night we stayed in the top house we took my cat Charlotte up with us. Mum had already moved our belongings and set up our new bedrooms; mine was the larger one adjacent to the kitchen, and Tanya's was a smaller room at the front of the house. As I carried Charlotte through the back entrance of the house, Tanya followed me up the rickety wooden steps. Suddenly, Charlotte leapt out of my arms and raced back to the main house. Tanya ran after her. After much coaxing and prying, we finally caught Charlotte. Holding her extra tight this time, we walked back up the rickety stairs into the top house.

As soon as we walked through the back door, Charlotte started to squirm. She wriggled this way and that, trying her hardest to get out of my arms. I'd never seen her do that. She was usually docile – perfectly happy being picked up and carried around. But now she was squirming fiercely and scratching me, desperate to get out of my arms.

I put Charlotte down and watched as she ran to the back door to escape, but Tanya had already closed it. Charlotte turned around to face the wall. The hair on the back of her neck slowly rose and she began to hiss and spit at the walls as if she were cornered. Her body was coiled tight like a spring, her teeth bared.

Tanya and I watched in horror as Charlotte then started swiping at the walls. It was as if she were attacking *invisible people*. We'd never seen her hiss or spit or snarl or bare her teeth before. But now she was scratching and swiping and howling and jumping up at things we couldn't hear or see; things that seemed to be either in the walls or just in front of them.

Tanya and I ran out the back door, yelling, 'Mum! Mum! Come quick!' When Mum walked in and saw Charlotte hissing and attacking the walls, she said, 'Let the poor cat out.' I opened the back door and Charlotte took off. She never came to the top house again. She already knew that something dark resided there, but it would take months before we'd be convinced of it too.

Tanya and I began to experience hauntings and super-natural occurrences that were even more disturbing than those we'd experienced on the Gold Coast. Doors opened and closed by themselves, loud footsteps stomped through the house at night when we were trying to sleep and eerie black shapes hung around, moving about the house. We also experienced physical attacks and being pushed by invisible forces.

Every night, Tanya would sleep on a mattress on my floor because if she slept in her room, she'd be woken by loud clanging noises next to her head. A presence would also push down on her and then try to lift her out of bed.

Despite this, one night Tanya tried to sleep in her own room . . .

On Friday she'd had a girlfriend stay over. They were up late and had crashed out in Tanya's room. I was working as a receptionist at Dad's surgery every Saturday morning, and was just getting home from work when I heard screams.

I raced inside and found Tanya in her room, along with my mum and my aunt. Tanya was screaming hysterically, 'Where did it come from? Why in my room? *Why has this happened to me!*'

I stepped inside and it was ice cold, as though I'd stepped into a refrigerator. Then I saw what the commotion was about. Tanya's entire room was covered in black dust.

It was everywhere. It was all over her bed, her books and clothes, as well as the ceiling, walls and windows. Absolutely everything was covered in a thin layer of black dust – her desk and schoolbooks and bags and cosmetics. I looked up at the ceiling. The dark powder had even settled on the large cobwebs up there, making her room look like a scene out of a horror movie.

Mum was trying to calm Tanya down. 'There's an explanation for all this. Don't worry. We'll find out why it happened. We will,' Mum kept consoling her. But I could tell by Mum's voice that she was shaken too.

My aunt was hurriedly trying to clean up the mess, but she was white in the face and clearly upset. She was a high school teacher who prided herself on her intelligence and rationality. For her, there was a logical explanation for everything, but even she knew there was no natural explanation for this – only a dark and unnatural one.

Whatever had caused the black dust in Tanya's room, it didn't want us living in the top house. We could all feel it. Right away, Tanya and I were moved back down into the main house.

We never talked about what had happened. Like the black dust, it was swept away.

CHAPTER 8

NEW ZEALAND

In 1996, I graduated from high school. Three months later, I left the house on the Central Coast behind, along with the terrifying incidents that had happened there.

By the time I finished school, a deep rift had begun to form between myself and my friends. I wanted to get away. I'd always felt different from other people there – more deep-thinking and sensitive – and now that I was done with school, I couldn't be bothered trying to fit in anymore. I wanted to leave. I knew I'd miss my mum and siblings, but I was tired of pretending to be someone else.

I wanted a new life, and I wanted to 'discover myself'. So, a few months after leaving school, I moved to New Zealand. I ended up staying there for ten months. It was one of the most powerful experiences I'd had in my life so far.

While I was there, I lived on a farm. I would spend hours walking by myself in the green fields, riding my motorbike out on the plains and tending to the animals and gardens. It was deeply healing. It was the first time I'd spent so much time alone in nature, and also the first time I realised how being connected to nature could heal you. There's something incredibly comforting about the steadiness of the natural world – how the cycles of life keep moving and the seasons keep changing, no matter what else is happening. I felt like I finally had a space where I could reflect upon my childhood and life and gain some perspective, even though I still saw ghosts and people's shadows, and kept having the frightening vision of the red-haired girl in chains.

In New Zealand, I experienced the freedom of not having a past. No one knew me; I felt like I could be anybody. I was eighteen, and I felt like I could change my life for good. I was finally free to think about who I wanted to be, and what type of life I wanted to live.

It was also in New Zealand that I discovered Tori Amos's music. I had first heard of her in Australia, not long before I graduated, when a classmate at school sang one of her songs, 'Winter', at assembly. I loved the song so much I went out and bought all her albums, and in New Zealand I spent many hours listening to them. With a headset on, drinking Baileys, I'd lose myself in her music. Something about the rawness and passion of her sound connected with me and made me feel understood. It changed and healed me, and made me want to create a new life.

I felt energised. New Zealand was the beginning of my path to deep, lasting healing. When I returned to Sydney in December 1997, I was a different person.

I enrolled in university and began a course in Media and Communications the following year. I hadn't yet properly dealt with my past or learned how to cope with my psychic abilities, but I felt hope. I was motivated and ambitious. I was the captain of my own ship; the creator of my destiny. I would grab life with both hands and mould and shape it to my *own* design.

And then I met a woman who had a slightly different forecast for me.

I'm sitting across the table from an astrologer. She's nice enough – polite and well spoken. Her house is cosy and charming. I've come to her to learn about Aura-Soma, but she's asked if she can look at my astrological chart.

I don't really believe in astrology, and have never done anything like this before. So as she goes on, reading my birth chart to me and telling me about my life and child-hood, I'm sceptical.

You'd think that with all the strange things I've experienced in my life, I would believe in astrology. But, truth be told, I'm a pragmatist. Until I get proof – tangible, evidence-based proof – until it happens to me or someone I know and trust, I don't believe it. Until then, it's just theory and fluff and woo-woo.

So far, what she's said about my childhood sounds accurate, but also generic. Yes, my childhood years were hard. Yes, I had a difficult relationship with my father. Yes, I felt lonely and isolated in my teens. And yes, I'm trying to figure out who I am and what I want to do with my life. But don't all teenagers feel that way?

'See here,' she says, pointing to a line on my birth chart – there are so many lines running up and down the page I don't know which line she means – 'this line indicates the near future, around the year 2000, and this shows me that in this year you'll experience a rebirth. In this year your old life will completely dissolve and a new life will begin.'

I stifle a sigh.

'In this year,' she continues, pointing to the line on the page again, 'a fire will sweep through your life, burning up everything that is old and outdated and needs to die. Then, like a phoenix rising from the ashes, you will be transformed.'

It was 1998, and supposedly in eighteen months' time, my new life was to start – after a massive fire. I didn't love the outlook, but I wasn't particularly worried; after all, I didn't put much stock in astrology, or in this woman's psychic talents.

But her prediction proved to be accurate.

CHAPTER 9

THE FIRE

When the astrologer predicted that a fire would sweep through my life, I didn't know she meant it literally. Perhaps she didn't either. But in July 2000, the main house burned to the ground.

My brother Aaron was minding the house while my parents were on vacation with Tanya and Rebekah. Aaron and his friends were cooking French fries on the stove, and the oil ignited with the gas. Within minutes, the entire kitchen was alight. The house was made entirely of timber, so the fire spread quickly. Within the hour, the whole house was on fire.

Years before, I'd seen visions of the house burning down. They'd started as soon as we moved back in, after we returned from the Gold Coast. I'd be walking through the house and suddenly I'd have a flash of it being on fire, or when I'd fall asleep at night, I'd see myself surrounded by a wall of red and yellow flames.

I knew it was a premonition, but I would brush it away or try to push down what I saw. I was frightened of my abilities; I never wanted to know about future events, like the fact that my primary school friend would die young (she died in her early twenties), or that another friend would contract a terminal illness (which happened when she was nineteen). I was terrified of what I saw because I still believed, even though it was years after we'd left the Pentecostal church, that I was bad and cursed.

But I wasn't the only one who had a feeling that something was very wrong with the house.

I'm lying on my futon reading through lecture notes from one of my classes at university. The phone rings; it's Mum. Her voice is edgy and strained.

'What's happened?' I ask her, feeling my pulse rise.

'Nothing,' she says, '. . . yet. But I'm worried about the house. I think the ghosts from the top house have come down to the main house. It feels dark and creepy. Something isn't right.'

I pause, taking it in. This is the first time she's talked like this, about the house, about ghosts. Or about the things I saw and experienced as a child. I'd never even heard her say the word 'ghost' before.

'I feel like the house is growing darkness,' she continues, 'spreading it. Something evil is living in our house

and I don't know what to do. It feels like bad spirits are trying to make the house dark in an attempt to push us out!'

I want to comfort her, tell her it's not true, but I can't, because I agree with her. The last few times I'd stayed there the energy in the house had been so heavy and dark that I'd gone to my boyfriend's parents' place for the night.

'Rebekah is having terrible nightmares and seeing scary shapes and shadows on the walls in her room,' Mum goes on. 'I keep trimming back the garden and the plants to let more light in, but it isn't working. I've been burning candles and praying, but that isn't working either. The house just seems to be getting darker! The bad energy is getting stronger. It feels like I'm in some spiritual battle, in spiritual warfare with the dark spirits. I'm scared something bad will happen if we don't leave! What should I do, Belinda?'

'I don't know, Mum.' I wish I can say something to help, to comfort her, but I'm at a loss.

I will never forget the day it happened. It was a Sunday afternoon, and I was at my boyfriend's parents' house on the Central Coast. A neighbour phoned to tell us that the main house was burning to the ground. They said Aaron had been in the house with his friends.

'He's in really bad shape,' my boyfriend said to me, relaying the news. 'He almost didn't get out in time. He made it just before the house exploded.'

When I finally reached Aaron on his mobile phone, he was crying so hard I couldn't understand what he was saying. Eventually I realised he was trying to tell me he hadn't been able to rescue our little cocker spaniel, Sam, before the explosion. I later learned that none of our pets – our dog and two cats – had survived.

It was almost too much for me to take. My parents and sisters were away and I didn't know what to do; I couldn't get hold of them to tell them what had happened. I started crying uncontrollably.

My boyfriend drove me to the house. From the top of the drive, as we made our way towards the house, we saw big, thick tendrils of black smoke rising from the ground, reaching far and wide into the sky. There were crowds of people and police and firemen everywhere. I frantically scanned the crowd for Aaron. Someone finally pointed him out to me and I ran towards him and hugged and cried with him.

Standing with Aaron were two firemen and a police officer, along with the friends who'd been in the house when the fire started. Aaron told me they were giving a statement. I left them and walked down the driveway to look at the burnt, wet mass that used to be our family home.

All that was left was a blackened and scorched frame where our house had stood. The fire had incinerated almost all the walls as well as our furniture and belongings, and everything had been scattered by the explosion. I couldn't even work out which room used to be my bedroom until I noticed the stinking, smouldering remains of my bed.

Together, my boyfriend and I walked down the side of the house to see if we could salvage anything from the charred wreckage. As we reached the end of the house, where Rebekah's bedroom used to be, a dark energy suddenly came rushing at me, shoving me backwards. It felt like a punch in the solar plexus, like the wind had been knocked out of me. Then something huge began bearing down upon me, pressing against me and trying to push me away.

My boyfriend's face, white and pinched, told me he felt it too. We fled back to his car, and as we ran, I could hear the voices of the bad spirits calling out to me, following me, chanting, mocking and menacing:

Ashes to ashes, dust to dust. Never come back . . .
Ashes to ashes, dust to dust. Never come back . . .
Ashes to ashes, dust to dust. Never come back . . .

I never did.

The house was only the first of our losses that year. After the house fire, Nanna Merle passed away. Then in October, Dad left Mum, ending their marriage of twenty-four years. Grandad George had passed away the year before. Even my relationship with my boyfriend ended.

Just as the astrologer had predicted, my life completely dissolved.

On top of all this, I suddenly became really unwell. I was vomiting all the time and had no idea why. There was a terrible burning feeling in the pit of my stomach; I was constantly nauseated and often couldn't sleep because of the pain.

Months later, I discovered I had an acute gastric ulcer – one of the worst the doctor had ever seen. I felt like the fire that had burned through my life, dissolving everything in its path, was burning me up from the inside too.

Unbelievably, it even seemed that my psychic, intuitive and empath gifts had become *stronger* again. I was now receiving so many impressions and taking on so many people's pain and illness that it was making me feel like I was going crazy. There seemed to be no protection at all anymore. My panic attacks became so bad that there were days I couldn't leave my apartment.

I didn't feel safe. *Anywhere.* Not out in public, not in my apartment. Not even in my own body.

I'd come into this life with fear, and every time I felt that things were getting better – that I'd turned a corner – everything fell apart again. I was trying so hard to have a happy life, but all my fears just kept compounding. I began to fantasise about how I might end my life. I'd imagine tying rocks to my feet and walking into the ocean, or taking a handful of pills and falling into a deep, dark sleep from which I'd never wake up.

One night, desperate and seriously considering suicide, I confessed to Mum. I told her about my physical sickness, panic and despair, and also about the things I was seeing.

'When I close my eyes,' I told her, 'I have this recurring vision. I see a red-haired girl with blue and black bruises, bound in chains. She's falling down out of the sky towards me. I don't know what it means. I haven't just been having this vision lately. I've had it for years. When I see this, when I see her falling towards me, I'm frightened, but I also feel like she is trying to tell me something.'

'Find a therapist,' Mum urged. 'Find someone you can talk to about it. I think the red-haired girl is trying to tell you something, and you need help.'

CHAPTER 10

THE DARK NIGHT

I took my mum's advice and found a therapist, and committed to seeing her twice a week. Right away, though, it was evident she wouldn't be able to help me.

I'm sitting in the therapist's office. It's our first visit, and she's introducing herself and telling me a bit about her approach. I'm listening, but something just next to her catches my eye. It's an older woman. A spirit. She's standing there waving to me.

'What are you looking at?'

I turn back to the therapist, who is looking at me expectantly. Do I tell her what I can see? In the past it's always gone wrong. I've been told I'm making it up, or that I should mind my own business, or that I'm crazy. But I really need help. Maybe I should open up to her?

I take a deep breath and say, 'I can see your deceased grandmother.'

The therapist frowns and exhales heavily. I recognise the disapproval in her manner, but she doesn't say anything. She's waiting to see what else I have to say.

I'm silent.

She shifts in her chair, then sighs. There's pity in her sigh. Or perhaps exasperation. I'm familiar with both.

'Belinda, in the course of this therapy you will come to realise that spirits aren't real; they are inner personalities — fictitious entities — that you have created in order to survive a difficult childhood . . .'

My heart drops — she doesn't believe me. I'm watching her lips move without sound. She can't help me. Here we go again.

'. . . so you could cope with the trauma you've experienced. You've made them up,' she's saying. 'Spirits aren't real; neither are ghosts. It's all in your imagination.'

She takes a deep breath and looks at me solidly as if she's just made a profound declaration that she's prepared to defend. My gaze drops to the floor and all I can think is, 'I wonder how many sessions I'll have to get through with this person to keep Mum from worrying about me?'

I'd been hopeful that the therapist would provide at least some relief from what I was experiencing, but it wasn't to be. Her reaction just made me feel even more isolated. My last vestiges of hope, the feeling that my life would change for the better, disappeared.

This time was truly the darkest in my life. These were the years in which I experienced what many refer to as a 'dark night of the soul'.

The fire that had swept through my life – through my house, through my family, through my solar plexus, through my psyche – incinerated everything I'd known and loved. It felt like I was experiencing the wrath of purgatory – *ashes to ashes, dust to dust* – and a new life, the new life the astrologer had promised me, was nowhere on the horizon. I was gazing into the abyss.

A dark night of the soul is beyond depression. It feels like the pain of it will never end, that the darkness will never lift. It can feel as though you're being punished for something, or like the entire purpose of your life is to suffer. You become the walking dead.

I was searching, clutching, trying to find solace and comfort and stability, but every time I reached for something, it dissolved like dust in my hands. Everything around me was grey and withering and dying.

It was earthbound hell.

But, like all cycles of life, like all deaths, rebirth does follow . . . just as the astrologer had predicted. Although I thought I would never be released from my inner darkness, the dark night of the soul does – inevitably – lead to release. We do come out of the pain to find the light.

At first, it's hard to see the brightness amidst all the dark; there are only the smallest, faintest splinters of light, like a tiny window atop a prison wall. But if we focus upon these splinters, however small and faint, eventually they grow into shafts of light, then those shafts become streams . . . And before you know it, the light is cracking through and pouring down on you. You're bathed in light and can see the new path ahead.

You've moved from dark to light.

The lessons of the dark night of the soul are among the hardest to learn because they are lessons of faith. In that space, the sense of despair is so heavy, the feeling of isolation so great that it's nearly impossible to imagine having faith in anything again. And yet that is what ultimately pulls you through. Those little shafts of light are messengers – reminders that you are not alone. That you can never be truly alone, because you can never be separated from your own divinity. You can never be separated from the source, from love, from light – from where we all originate.

It seems backwards, finding love and connection in the midst of such darkness. But somehow, when all else is gone, you come to realise the only thing left is that which can never be destroyed – your eternal spirit.

As you begin to know this, not just with your mind but also with your body and soul, you begin to heal.

My life fell apart in the year 2000 – literally, in many respects. After that, I lost all hope; I was ready to give up. But when I finally stopped trying, when I finally stopped pushing for an answer to the question of why all this had happened to me, I got one.

My dark night of the soul had begun with the dissolution of my family, but it came full circle and ended with a healing of my family – a message from Grandma Jean.

I'm sitting on my bed trying to study for an anthropology exam, but I'm distracted. I'd rather be heading into town and meeting up with a girlfriend for lunch, but I need to cram.

I glance out the window and see a neighbour across the road trimming her rose bush. She looks lovely in her white cotton dress and gloves, with her long, silver-grey hair pulled back into a bun.

She sees me and waves from across the street. I wave back, wanting to go out and chat with her — anything to spare me from having to learn about the symbolism of ancient Australian Aboriginal cave paintings — but I make myself stay.

I turn the page and begin reading when suddenly a voice speaks to me. Clear and loud, it says, 'Put down that book and listen to me!'

I freeze. I know it's the voice of a spirit because it says things I wouldn't say or know, but I've never heard a spirit voice come through so audibly. Usually when spirits speak to me, I hear them inside my head; they sound like my own internal voice, although I know it's not my voice. But this spirit is audible and loud, which makes me afraid.

'Belinda, don't be scared. It's your Grandma Jean. I need to talk to you!'

I sit bolt upright. I'm still scared, but I know this must be important.

Grandma Jean had seven children — five sons and two daughters. She begins to tell me about one of her sons.

She's telling me private and intimate things about him, secret things too – things that happened before I was born. I don't understand why she's telling me any of this, or what I'm supposed to do with this information.

But then Grandma Jean urges me to contact my uncle and tell him what she's told me. He needs to know she loves him and that she is worried about him. It is urgent that I contact him immediately.

Clearly Grandma is worried, but I don't want to contact my uncle. I hardly know him, and I'm scared he'll think I'm crazy. Also, I promised my new therapist that I wouldn't listen to the voices anymore. I need to learn to ignore them, to push them away and quiet them, and listening to Grandma Jean's voice may bring them all flooding back in. I want to be normal, not crazy.

I won't contact him, I decide.

As soon as I make this decision, her voice booms so loud that my head shakes. 'BELINDA! YOU WILL CONTACT HIM!'

Two hours later I was speaking to my uncle on the phone. He wasn't scared about what I told him, nor did he think I was crazy. He was understandably shocked, but also deeply moved.

Unbeknown to me and my family, he had been struggling with depression for years, and had been thinking about ending his life. By getting me to reach out to him and relay her message, Grandma Jean had saved his life.

My uncle had never been able to share the pain of his depression with another person, but now there was hope.

I understood him. His mother understood him. Somebody cared. He didn't want to end his life anymore, and in the years after that phone call, he, with the help of a beautiful woman (who would later become his wife), was able to heal from his depression and live a happy life.

I cannot overstate the impact of that day. It changed *everything* for me, forever. It was the first time something good had come from my abilities. I'd thought I was cursed and that I needed to hide myself. But, for the first time, I had brought light into someone's life through *sharing* myself.

When I ended the phone call, Grandma Jean patted me on the shoulder and said, 'Remember, dear child, I told you that when you grew up it would be different. See – there is a reason you have these gifts. You can help others. It's time to begin!'

And I did.

CHAPTER 11

GERMANY

Finally, I had been released from the dark night of my soul. I realised that the abilities that had burdened me for so long were gifts; now I just needed to learn how to use them. But life had to take me away from the country of my birth for this to happen.

The year before, I'd been visiting my father at a remote Aboriginal community where he'd been working as a Flying Doctor. On the red-eye flight from Darwin back to Sydney I sat next to a man from Germany. Nine months later, I immigrated to Germany to be with him, and it was there that my career as an intuitive began.

I was smitten with Germany the moment I laid eyes upon it. As we made our descent into Frankfurt Airport, flying low over the countryside, I fell in love with its green fields and forests, and its quaint villages and churches, with their sloping roofs and medieval architecture. There was something so mystical about Germany, so Gothic and fairytale-like.

But there was also something deeper than that. When I stepped off the plane and onto European soil, I was hit by the strongest sense that I was home again. I had *returned.* I had come back to where I belonged.

Yet this feeling of deep connection and homecoming was also tinged with angst. I couldn't help feeling like something bad and old had happened to me here. As I walked through Frankfurt Airport, then went through passport control and waited for my luggage, my heart was racing and I was sweating profusely. I knew life had brought me here to blossom, to throw off the shackles of my past and create a new life, but I found myself filled with trepidation . . . Did this mean further and deeper (and probably more painful) healing?

In the following months, this all proved true . . . Something bad and old *had* happened to me in Germany: my past lives.

I'm standing in the queue at the supermarket checkout.

Abruptly, everything around me disappears. I'm no longer at the store, I'm in the past. In another era. When I go to move, I feel the bindings — I can't move my body or my hands. I'm tied to a post!

Suddenly I'm surrounded by a circle of fire. I scream and struggle, trying desperately to free myself, but the fire's moving too quickly. It's closing in on me. I can feel the heat on my body. Now my flesh is starting to scorch and burn. It's melting off me like wax . . .

I blink, and I'm back in the store, clutching my groceries and breathing hard. I drop everything and run. Everyone stares after me.

I race to my apartment. It's only minutes away, thank goodness — I only just make it before the vision returns and overtakes me. I'm on the ground sobbing. I'm burning! They're killing me because I'm a witch!

I'm shaking, shocked and overwhelmed. But I also have a sense that this vision is trying to tell me something.

Days after this first vision of one of my past lives, I was out walking along the Rhine River when another struck me. This time, I was being dragged out of bed in the middle of the night by a group of men, then jailed, beaten and hanged. Another time, I was renounced by my family at a public hearing, then tortured and drowned for being a witch.

Over the course of several months, I relived roughly twenty of my past lives. They would appear suddenly, out of nowhere, and overtake me. Each time, I'd find myself re-experiencing another trauma — another death, murder, beating or hanging.

It took me some time to realise that what I was experiencing were visions of my past lives. I'd heard about reincarnation, but I didn't know if I believed in the notion of past lives. I'd also never heard of anyone spontaneously re-experiencing their own.

Even though I'd begun to understand what I was seeing, not knowing when the visions would hit was incredibly stressful.

Eventually I worked out how to hold them off. When I felt a vision coming on, I would block it as much as I could until I made it home, where I would relive it entirely. Many times

I had to flee the language school where I was learning German so I could get home, crawl under my duvet and allow the vision to come through.

I didn't know why I was reliving my past lives, but somehow I intuitively knew I needed to let them come forth so I could learn what had happened to me.

Before long, it started to become clear – the lives I was being shown all had a central theme. Over and over I had been persecuted for my psychic and intuitive abilities. Sometimes I was called a 'witch' or a 'heretic' and was tried and murdered for my gifts. Other times it happened less publicly; I was abandoned, or punished by one of my parents, cast out of my village or rejected by my family because I was 'different'.

I didn't always die painfully because of what I could see or do, but I was *never safe to be myself.* And I came to realise that I was suffering this again in my present life because I was still carrying the unhealed trauma of these past-life persecutions.

But while the experience of reliving my past lives was unpleasant, and at times downright frightening, it was also liberating. For the first time ever, my childhood made sense. I now understood how the Law of Resonance works: *Your past will become your future unless you heal it.* Throughout my childhood I had unconsciously attracted persecution and pain because I hadn't healed the persecution and pain from my past lives. My present life was a reflection of my past!

I also understood why I'd been led to immigrate – return – to Germany. Europe was not only my long-lost love, it was also my long-lost pain. I had returned to the core of my pain so it could be purged and healed.

I felt inspired to heal my old wounds so I wouldn't have to deal with the lingering effects of the persecution anymore. This experience urged me to heal whatever was holding me back from accepting my abilities.

For the first time ever, I was ready to embrace my psychic, intuitive and empath abilities fully. It was time to learn how to use them.

CHAPTER 12

FORTUNE-TELLING

Before moving to Germany, I had done a little exploring of my talents. For a few months, I had worked in a psychic cafe on the Central Coast, where I was paid to read people's fortunes. It certainly wasn't my dream job, but after what had happened with Grandma Jean and my uncle, I knew I had to begin somewhere.

To apply for the job, I was asked to bring my own tarot deck and give the owner of the cafe a reading. I had a pack of tarot cards, but I didn't know how to read them; there had never been any point – I didn't need cards to read someone. I figured I'd just shuffle the cards, place them on the table and pretend I could read them while reading her energy field and chakras instead. No problem.

When I arrived for the interview, my heart sank. Covering the walls and windowsills were pictures and figurines of fairies, elves, ascended masters and Native Americans, all jammed in among crystals, wands, runes and silver pentagrams. I had arrived on Planet Woo-Woo!

The owner of the cafe came gliding out to meet me. She was in her late fifties, dressed in a long, emerald-green, Egyptian-style robe with a matching silver headpiece and necklace. Her badly dyed black hair was pulled back in a tight bun and her eyes were heavily made up with black and blue eye shadow, as if she believed herself to be the reincarnation of Cleopatra.

But it wasn't so much her looks as her air of spiritual arrogance that made me dislike her instantly. Holding out a bejewelled hand, she ushered me over to a small table at the front of the cafe and told me to get started. She sat herself down and looked at me expectantly.

'Okay,' I say, trying to remember what the tarot book had said. Right – I'm supposed to shuffle the deck.

I shuffle the cards around in my hands for a few moments, then cut the deck.

Wait, what's next? Do I tap the cards to infuse them with our energies, or do I lay the spread first?

My heart starts beating faster.

I think I need to tap the cards, but was it supposed to be with my left hand or my right? The book was really specific, but I can't remember. And hold on – does she lay the cards, or do I?

This is a disaster! I'm sure at this point she can tell I have no idea what I'm doing.

I glance up. Cleopatra is staring at me, eyebrows raised, clearly unimpressed. I start to shuffle again, but she places a hand on the table, signalling for me to stop.

'Do you know how to read tarot, Belinda?' she says.

My shoulders drop. 'No,' I sigh. 'I don't know how to read tarot. But I do know how to read people. Here – give me your hand. I'll show you.'

She's wary, but slowly she offers me her hand. I take it in mine, close my eyes and, just like that, the tiny movies and colours start flashing, and I can feel what she's feeling. For the next half hour, I tell her all about herself.

When I'm finished, I open my eyes and see that she's crying. Her face is blotchy and her entire demeanour has changed; she's now meek and soft. Slowly she slips her hand from mine, reaches into her bra and pulls out a sparkly purple handkerchief.

'My dear,' she sniffs, 'you don't need tarot cards to read people. I don't know how you knew all that about me, but you have a gift. I've never seen that type of talent before.' She takes a moment to dab at her smudged eyes, then continues. 'But in this cafe, people don't want to hear about the troubles in their lives. They come here because they want relief from them. If you work here, you will need to read people's fortunes, because that is what they pay for. Do you understand? You have to read their futures and give them hope.'

85

Right from the start, I hated telling people their futures. I wasn't telling them everything I could see about them; I shared only what would *probably* happen in their lives.

At any moment in time, there are many paths stretched out in front of us, many probabilities of how our futures *could* unfold. Whatever choices we make in the present moment influence our futures; we can shape and choose our destinies. But I wasn't supposed to tell people this – I was paid to predict only one future.

I did my best to find the most *probable* path in a person's future. People seemed pleased with the futures I predicted for them, most likely because I was telling them what they wanted to hear.

I became very popular at the cafe, but I felt ashamed. I tried to ease my guilt by reminding myself that most psychics simply told people what they wanted to hear. But even so, I felt like a fake. When I left Australia to live in Germany, I decided I would never work as a fortune-teller again.

I was also having doubts about whether I wanted to work as a psychic; I didn't fit into the 'psychic scene'. Most readers were at least thirty years older than me. They all seemed to have attractive, younger Native American spirit guides and, by some coincidence, all happened to have been famous people, queens or goddesses in their past lives as well. At that time in my life, it seemed to me that spirituality largely boiled down to the fantasies of bored middle-aged women.

But I was a realist and a critical thinker, and that all felt like fantasy to me, far removed from people's *real* life issues.

I couldn't help but think: What is the point of having psychic gifts if you can't use them in a *real* way to help people with their real-life issues? I kept searching, sure there must be another way to use my abilities. I was determined to find it.

CHAPTER 13

MEDIUMSHIP TRAINING

I didn't want to be a fortune-teller and I didn't fit into the psychic scene – that much was certain. But I still felt guided to pursue the path of developing my psychic abilities.

I had always seen spirits, so I thought perhaps I could try working as a medium. (A medium is someone who speaks to spirits – deceased people – and passes on messages to their loved ones.)

All my life I'd been communicating with spirits – I knew I could do it. Eighteen months earlier, I'd spoken to my grandmother and what she had to say transformed her son's life. Perhaps relaying messages from the Other Side could bring peace and comfort to others too?

So in 2002, I flew from Germany to England to attend a six-day mediumship course. I was unsure what to expect.

Would we be communicating with spirits who had returned home, or with ghosts who hadn't yet found the light and made the transition?

Truth be told, I was just as eager to help ghosts and spirits as their living loved ones. Since moving to Germany and reliving my past lives, my experiences with ghosts had started to change. I was still seeing them most nights, and they would still crowd in on me and want to talk with me, but somehow it wasn't as scary as before. They would no longer touch me or compete for my attention. I was starting to realise they didn't want to harm me. They weren't scary or menacing, just desperate for help.

What I didn't know at the time was that I was growing stronger energetically. My energy field was becoming larger, more luminous, which meant ghosts could no longer have 'access' to me whenever they wanted, or grab or attack me.

There were other positive effects too. I was still attuned to see people's shadows and to know what was wrong with them, and I was still a ghost whisperer, but I was no longer experiencing the suffering these abilities had caused me in the past. I was less fearful, more resilient and better protected. This in turn made me much less afraid of my abilities, and much more motivated to start using them. Healing my past lives was healing my shadow, and this was helping me embrace my light.

As I set out for England, I hoped this course would be the beginning of a career where I could use my abilities. And that is exactly what happened – just not in the way I'd thought. I arrived at the course full of excitement, expecting to acquire the practical skills I'd needed to work as a medium. But by the close of the first day I had learned just one thing – that mediumship was not for me.

I was disappointed to learn that mediumship did not involve helping ghosts. But I was even more disappointed (and shocked) by the state of poor health of the mediums running the course.

The five mediums who taught and tutored us were all in terrible health. I didn't need my abilities to see that; it was apparent to everyone. All three of the female tutors were so overweight that they struggled to walk across the room. Both of the male tutors, although only in their fifties, already used crutches. One of them could barely talk, and he could do little more than hobble, having been struck down with a mystery virus that had paralysed his face and body.

On the first day of the course we were told that he'd contracted the disease because mediumship work is taxing on the body; it makes you weak and vulnerable. We were told this could also happen to us, and that the way to protect ourselves was to 'ground' ourselves by being overweight.

The tutors told us that the *very* best and most gifted mediums were obese. I watched in shock as my fellow course participants nodded and accepted this. I couldn't help but wonder if they'd have been as agreeable if they, too, could look inside the tutors and see their liver problems, their developing diabetes and osteoporosis, their fatigue and mental fogginess and exhaustion.

When we were told that this state was a necessary part of being a medium I immediately thought, 'No thanks!' I also just wasn't vibing with what we were learning.

I could easily see, communicate with and pass on messages from the Other Side, but somehow it didn't feel right. Many of my fellow students were loving the course. They quickly developed their abilities and thrived in their newfound roles as mediums. But for some reason, I didn't share their passion.

The morning session is packed. Fifty or more people are in the meeting room, excited and anxious as they prepare to take their turns giving live demonstrations.

One by one, students get up in front of the group and start relaying messages from our dead relatives and friends. Everyone seems so happy doing this . . . except me.

I can't help it. I'm trying to get into it. I have no trouble seeing spirits or hearing their messages, but it just doesn't feel right. It's not for me.

I'm starting to fidget. What am I doing here? And if this doesn't work, what will I do? I already know I don't want to be a fortune-teller. So what's left?

Forget it. I slip out the rear door unnoticed and head upstairs to my room, where I throw myself down on the bed. The tears come quickly.

The course is over tomorrow and then what? I can't stop being psychic. I can't make it all go away, so why is this happening? I was sure I'd been guided here, to this course . . .

I sit up and take a deep breath. That's it – I'm done. I'll skip the evening session and catch a taxi to the airport in the morning.

As soon as I decide this I hear a familiar voice, loud and clear.

'Go downstairs and attend the evening session,
Belinda. It will all work out, I promise.'
It's my Grandma Jean. By now I know better than to
ignore what she's telling me. I drag myself off the bed and
leave my room.

I didn't understand why Grandma Jean had urged me to continue, why she'd sent me downstairs, but I went. During the evening session we were to work in pairs, connecting to the Other Side and communicating with any deceased loved ones who may come through. I was partnered with an elderly man who had a kind, open face and green eyes.

My partner, who could tell from my swollen, red eyes that I'd been crying, gently walked me out of the room and down the hall, looking for a quiet place for us to talk. He found a comfy couch and sat me down, and I poured out my heart to him.

When I finished, he said, 'So, if you don't want to be a medium and relay messages from the Other Side, and if you don't know what you want to do, what *can* you do? How do you read people?' Like I had done with the owner of the psychic cafe, I reached over and took his hand. The images and colours appeared, and I started telling him about himself.

I told him everything about his life, his struggles and dreams. Then, starting at his feet and working my way up his body, I told him every health problem that was ailing him.

When I finished, his eyes were wide and his mouth hung open like a fish. He was in a state of shock. As it turned out, he was a medical doctor and a doctor of osteopathy. Not only was

I completely accurate in my diagnosis, but the information I had given him was also highly specific and detailed. He kept spluttering and shaking his head, saying, 'Simply incredible! Absolutely, simply incredible!'

He told me I didn't need to worry about not wanting to work as a medium because I was a 'medical intuitive'. I'd never heard the term before. He asked me if I'd heard of Caroline Myss and her work, and I told him I hadn't.

'They sell her books here, Belinda. Right here in the college. You must purchase them!' As soon as the store opened the following day, I bought two of her books – *Anatomy of the Spirit* and *Why People Don't Heal and How They Can*. I read them both cover to cover.

Finally, I had discovered what I was: *a medical intuitive*. Not only was there a term to describe what I could do – perceiving what was wrong with people – but I could also make a career from it!

Caroline Myss didn't read people's futures or talk to dead people; she told people what was wrong with them. *She used her gifts to help people in a real way with their real-life issues.* This was the piece of my life-puzzle I'd been looking for.

I was on my way.

CHAPTER 14

MEDICAL INTUITION

After I returned to Germany, I told a few people about my ability to 'see inside' people. They asked if I would do sessions for them, and I did. Afterwards, they told their friends about me, and things quickly grew from there. Within three years I had a solid reputation as a medical intuitive.

People from countries all around the world started to consult with me about all kinds of problems: why they were unwell or feeling depressed; why they were struggling in their marriage or with their children; why they were tired or lacking passion; why they couldn't find the right career or figure out their life purpose. In time, doctors and other medical professionals heard about my abilities and started coming to me for sessions too. And then they started consulting me for help with their patients.

I would conduct these sessions in my apartment in Germany, or via the telephone. I don't have to be in the same room as someone to read them – I can see and feel people's energy from thousands of miles away. At the start of every session, I'd relay to people their past-life histories and problems. I didn't know if other psychics or medical intuitives worked this way, but I found it incredibly helpful. I'd learned through my own experiences that past-life issues can become present-life challenges.

Offering past-life readings to my clients not only showed me *exactly* what negative subconscious patterns they brought into this life, it also showed me *how* those negative subconscious patterns were causing struggles and conflicts. The past lives would give me volumes of information about a person's current life – about their health, relationships, creative ventures, family life and career.

After I'd read someone's past lives, I'd scan their body, reading their health and illnesses. I would always start at the feet and work my way up, simply because it felt right to do so.

Caroline Myss's books talked a lot about chakras, which are invisible wheels of energy located throughout the body and in the head. She used chakras to determine what wasn't working in people's bodies. Chakras didn't seem important to me at the time – my exploration of people's past lives gave me all the information I needed. Of course, I was already reading people's energy fields and the seven chakras within them, I just didn't know it yet.

After I'd scanned their body, people could ask me questions. This was their first opportunity to do so; at the start of every session, I asked clients *not* to tell me about themselves or why they sought my help. I wanted it to be clear that all the information I received was through my psychic and intuitive channels.

After I completed the reading, clients would usually ask me about their relationships, their career choices, their purpose in life or their finances. Often people would ask me about a deceased loved one, and I'd be able to make contact and speak to their family or friends on the Other Side. Though they often asked, I avoided answering questions about the future.

Initially, my sessions would last roughly two hours. Eventually, they became shorter as I started to find the core reason (or reasons) for a person's ill health or life problems more quickly. But I always worked in the same order, starting with a past-life reading, then scanning their energy field and chakras and finally answering their questions.

A woman named Monika is on the telephone. She's sixty years old and lives in Switzerland. I'm struggling to understand her. Though I speak German fluently by now, her Swiss German is difficult for me to understand. I can see her energy field perfectly, though, and besides, it's my job to do the talking.

I start the session by explaining to Monika how I work and, just as importantly, how I don't work.

'I don't work as a doctor and I'm not a healthcare practitioner, so I don't diagnose people's physical or mental conditions. It's important that you understand that what I'm about to tell you about yourself and your energy field is based upon the impressions I receive by working as an intuitive and spiritual coach. While I'm not a doctor, I do

work together with many doctors, and if I feel you have a healthcare concern that needs medical attention, I will happily refer you to one of them.

'What I also don't do is work as a fortune-teller. I do not believe in fortune-telling or future-predicting. I believe we create our own destinies, and it is my job as an intuitive to help you create the destiny you want by pointing out to you what isn't working in your life.

'It's important that you understand my role.' I pause again, wanting to emphasise this point. 'My job is to show you, to highlight to you, to talk to you about what isn't working in your life so that you can get it working.'

Monika will likely be more receptive to this idea than many of my native English-speaking clients. I've found that culturally Europeans and German-speaking people want to hear about what isn't working in their lives, but if I don't stress this point to native English speakers – Australians, New Zealanders, Americans and the British – they can become disappointed with the session because they think I've only focused on the negative.

I explain to Monika that I will look at her past-life history, which will help reveal what past-life patterns and subconscious belief systems are affecting her present life.

'It isn't important who you were or what you did in your past lives,' I say, 'but it is important to know what happened to you and how this made you believe what you do about your life. I need to find those negative, limiting and life-depleting subconscious belief systems within your past. I need to go to the root of them, so that we can find *them, dig them up and discard them, and then replace them with positive, limitless and life-affirming belief systems. Because what you believe about life, consciously or subconsciously, creates your reality.'*

I explain that I will then look at her energy field, working my way from her feet up and looking for block-ages, stagnations and pockets of disruption in the flow of energy – or chi – in her energy field. I will also be looking for health problems. After that, she may ask me questions.

Monika says she understands this, and the session begins. I take a deep breath and open my channels. It's like opening the floodgates. All my senses – sight, taste, touch, hearing, smell – are bombarded with feelings, visions and impressions. I let it come, let it wash over me in large waves of energy and information, which then begin to sort them-selves into a type of map or plan. In my mind's eye I see it all moving around, putting itself in order. The problems and issues and shadows are lining up for me to understand what they are.

I see Monika as a young man on a ship bound for England. She's wearing a dark-coloured cap and trousers and she's clutching onto the side of the ship, white-faced and looking out at the treacherous sea. The waves are huge, black and rolling, and the captain is telling everyone to hold on so they can make it through the storm, but Monika knows – the boy she was in that life knows – that her life will most likely end here tonight.

And it does. A crack of lightning lights up the sea for a terrible second and she sees a huge dark wall of water moving towards her. It crashes against the boat, capsizing it. Monika is thrown into the freezing water, and she drowns amidst the confusion and terror.

'The first thing I see is that you have a fear of the ocean and of swimming,' I say. 'You think this is an irrational fear, because you didn't have any bad experiences with water in your childhood.'

'Oh my goodness,' she gasps. 'This is true. I've always been scared of the ocean and when I was a small child and my family took me to the sea, I wouldn't go in. I wouldn't even put my toe in. My sisters would tease me about it.'

I explain her past-life experience to her. 'Now you know where this fear comes from,' I say, 'and you also know it isn't irrational. You have drowned before and your body – the cells of your body – remember this. But now that you know this, you can let it go. It happened then, but you can release yourself from it now.'

'I'm so relieved to find out that I'm not crazy!' Monika cries.

I laugh, understanding very well what it feels like to be afraid you're crazy.

'But this isn't the most important thing I want to tell you about this past life,' I continue. 'The main problem you have in your life is that you're terrified to step out of your comfort zone and take any risks. Your past experiences have taught you that adventure and trying something new leads to failure and pain. This has happened in many of your past lives.

'In this past life where you drowned, you had taken a shot at a new life. Everyone had warned you that it wouldn't work out, but you felt it was the right thing regardless. You were yearning for a new life; you needed change. But it didn't turn out well. So now you're afraid of your pioneering spirit because you don't trust your own judgement.'

I tell Monika that she was once imprisoned for marrying the man she loved, that she was rejected by her family for moving to another town, that she died of hunger and starvation on a trip to the desert, that she was robbed and beaten when walking alone into town at night. I continue, listing experience after experience that has contributed to her present fears.

Monika's past-life history of being punished for trying something new had led her subconscious mind to try to protect her from further hurts by leading her to avoid change – but this was making her bitterly unhappy. Monika's fear of change had caused her to marry her first boyfriend, stay in the village in which she'd grown up, take up the same profession as her mother (teacher) and not travel as much as she wanted. Monika was still a pioneer at heart, someone who needed to expand her horizons and explore new things. I could see that she felt she was *drying up* and *dying* inside.

As soon as I began Monika's body scan, I saw a dullness in both her first and second chakras – *the base chakra, the sacral chakra* – the chakras responsible for grounding, a sense of belonging, passion and joy. Monika had no passion, and as a result, she had an array of gynaecological issues. Working my way up from her feet to her legs to her lower abdomen, I saw that she had recurring bladder infections, back problems and had had a partial hysterectomy. I also saw that she experienced constant pain and discomfort in her vagina and pelvic area, and that when she was younger she'd had two abortions.

Monika's husband had told her to terminate the pregnancies because he was worried they couldn't afford a child. I also saw that her recurring bladder problems were because she was having intercourse with her husband when she didn't want to.

It was also apparent to me that Monika didn't like where she lived; she didn't feel at home there. Her secret fantasy was to live in the tropics. On one of the rare holidays she'd taken, she'd fallen in love with the sun and the warmth and the humidity. She'd never felt so good, and with her teacher's pension she could now afford to buy a small holiday house there. But her husband didn't like her being away, and she didn't like displeasing him. It was clear to me that Monika felt trapped in her life because she felt trapped in her marriage.

As I moved further up her body to her stomach and digestive areas, to the region of her third chakra – *the solar plexus* – I saw that she often had an upset stomach and felt nauseous. This wasn't only because she was afraid of her husband; it was also because she hated him. I could see anger and rage trapped in her stomach, and this anger and rage was giving her heartburn and indigestion.

There was more: Monika also hated herself. Some of that anger and rage she was feeling was directed inwards. She felt she was weak and lacked backbone. She detested her own fear and passivity, and this self-hate was making her digestive issues worse.

'Yes, this is true,' Monika told me. 'I hate this about myself and I wish I could change it. I don't want to be this way.'

'You are this way because you subconsciously fear change,' I said, trying to console her. 'In your past lives you've experienced suffering and tragedy whenever you dared to make a change or be different. Your subconscious mind remembers this, and those memories are keeping you small and afraid. Don't be too hard on yourself; don't add more hate to the hate you're already experiencing. Let me look further at your body, and then we can talk about what you can do.'

When I moved up into Monika's heart and chest region, the area of her *heart chakra*, I saw a heart murmur, as well as sadness and grief. Monika had been attending therapy for many years and had been taking antidepressants. I also saw that she felt lonely during the day. She had asked her husband for a pet, a dog or cat to care for, but he had refused. I saw that her husband was very traditional in his thinking. He could go to work and do as he pleased in the evenings, attending his clubs and social events, but she was supposed to stay at home and wait for him, giving him her full attention (and body) whenever he wanted. It was easy to understand why Monika was so unhappy.

When I moved up into her throat – *the throat chakra* – I saw that Monika often lost her voice because she was afraid to speak out against her husband, and when I looked at her brain, her sixth and seventh chakras – *the third eye chakra, the crown chakra* – I saw that it was underused. Monika was a witty and intelligent woman, a natural academic, but she did nothing to feed her eager mind.

We discussed how Monika could become more aware of the past-life patterns that were keeping her stuck in order to overcome them. As the session ended, Monika seemed uplifted and determined to change. I felt confident she would become more mindful of how her past was affecting her present, and would step away from her attitudes of scarcity and smallness.

Sessions like Monika's were typical; I could see an incredible level of detail about people's past lives and how they were creating physical and emotional challenges in their current lives. Working with people in this way – helping them to understand what forces were at play in their lives – was very fulfilling.

I worked full-time as a medical intuitive until 2007, when I was twenty-eight years old. I had a booming practice in Germany, and enjoyed wonderful relationships with doctors and healthcare practitioners.

I loved the connection with people and the way I could shed light on their troubles. I felt honoured and blessed to be able to do this work.

But I was harbouring a secret: I didn't feel that being a medical intuitive was my *soul purpose*. I *did* want to help people, but I still felt there was something else out there for me.

CHAPTER 15

THE VIBRATIONAL SPECTRUM

As the years went on, I enjoyed my work less and less. The sessions had become increasingly taxing and I was losing my passion for it. I felt guilty about the way I was feeling; I'd been given these abilities to help people. I should feel grateful. Still, as the days went by it became more apparent to me that medical intuition was only a stepping stone towards my life purpose. I was ready to find the next step.

I was also becoming disillusioned by my profession. I could see the root cause of my clients' problems, but I didn't know how to help them bring about a permanent change. I knew what needed to be healed, but not how.

The excellent medical professionals, therapists and alternative practitioners I was surrounded by – people at the top of their game in the healing profession – were struggling with this too. Our clients would consult us repeatedly with the same issues, but we didn't know how to resolve them.

And I didn't know how to heal myself, either. Like many of my clients and colleagues, I didn't have excellent health and wasn't feeling much joy in life. I was creatively blocked and unhappy.

I was in a funk, and although the acute ill health and torment of my childhood and teen years had lessened, I found myself lacking passion and purpose. I still had constant digestive problems, and to some extent I still took on other people's negative feelings and emotions. I was dragging myself through each day, and just didn't feel *alive*.

During my years as a medical intuitive, as dedicated as I was to my work, a niggling feeling stayed with me. It sat small in the pit of my stomach and whispered: *Medical intuition isn't your life purpose. Something else awaits.* And in August 2007, after many months of declining health and feeling completely burnt out, I decided to listen to that niggling voice. I had to discover what else was out there for me, and I had an idea of where to start.

A friend had recently told me about Eckhart Tolle's book *The Power of Now*. In one passage, Tolle says that if we're confused and lost and seeking life direction, we can find it by accessing the power of the present moment. Reading this, I instantly knew that was what I needed to do – to find direction and purpose by getting quiet and listening to my inner self. I decided to sit and wait until I discovered my life purpose.

So I took a month off. For weeks, I spent almost all day every day sitting in my white chair in my white office being 'present'. And it was while I was meditating that it happened . . .

I was sitting there, still, my mind restful, when suddenly I was outside of myself, standing and watching my 'other' self meditating.

It was shocking yet, strangely, it wasn't unnerving. I didn't feel scared or unsettled; in fact, I felt marvellous! I suddenly felt completely relieved of any burden of thought or ailment.

Around me and within me was a pervasive sense of stillness, peace and expansiveness. There were no thoughts in my mind. There were no emotions in my body. I felt completely free, and for the first time ever, I felt completely alive.

While I stood there, in bliss, watching myself meditate, I noticed that I was comprised of two parts, or two selves: a dark-self and a light-self. My dark- and light-selves were polar opposites.

My dark-self (my egoic self, which is fearful, anxious and insecure) existed right alongside my light-self (my spirit, which is loving, brave and wise). I'm unsure of how I suddenly knew these things, but somehow I did.

And in the moment that I understood this, in the moment that I realised I consisted of *equal parts* dark and light, I began to experience the dark as well as the light, within me . . .

It started as an experience of the vibration of *pure dark*. Suddenly I was plummeting down, down, down, headfirst into the deep dark depths of low vibration. A part of me remained sitting in the white chair in my office, but another part began to plummet. Somehow I knew I was headed into the bowels of the human experience – the lowest of the low and the darkest of dark, to the lowest end of the spectrum – but strangely, I didn't feel afraid. I knew I was learning an important life lesson, and that I needed to experience the vibration of pure dark. I allowed myself to plummet.

When I landed at the bottom of this spectrum, when I arrived at the complete and total suffocating blackness of the vibration of *pure dark*, I felt only dread. This was a feeling of hopelessness and desperation; a dark and grasping fear of annihilation, pain and despair.

It was suffocating, engulfing, debilitating. Malignant, woeful, doomful. It was utter despair and utter depression. *It was non-life.*

These dreadful feelings didn't overwhelm me, though. They were *external* to me – I didn't feel them as my own emotions. I felt them around me.

Before I had time to process all this, I found myself moving upwards. I was being gently lifted, pulled up beyond the vibration of pure dark, moving above it.

Finally, I came to rest. Here in this new, higher place, there wasn't the same blackness or feeling of complete doom. This vibration also felt dark and suffocating, but it wasn't as dark. The teeny, tiny sliver of light here told me I'd moved up a level.

In this place I felt depression and grief and self-hate. It wasn't utter despair and desperation like before – it wasn't complete *non-life* – but the vibration of this place was still deeply negative and fearful. This was the vibration of deep depression and suicidal feelings. But once again, before I had time to think or experience more about this vibration, I found myself being lifted up . . .

When I arrived at the next vibration, I instantly experienced the emotion of unworthiness. The vibration of this place seemed to be of a deep lack of self-esteem and self-worth. Here were feelings of lowliness, shame and degradation. Here were also feelings of self-reproach.

Suddenly, in a flash, I received an insight. I saw that many people get trapped at this low level of vibration – many people experience this dark, negative emotion – because they dislike themselves. I saw that disliking ourselves is a dangerous thing to do, and that all the violence in the world, all the atrocities and sufferings stem from our inability to love ourselves. It was a massive revelation, but once again, before I could think further about it, I found myself being lifted higher . . .

As things shifted yet again, I started to understand that I was being moved up a vibrational spectrum of sorts, from the darkest of the dark to the lighter shades of the dark. With every rise, I saw and experienced more light; I had started in blackness, but now was experiencing shades of grey. I had also moved further away from negative emotions and closer to positive ones.

The next vibration I was lifted to was of anger, bitterness and remorse. I also sensed guilt, jealousy and revenge. This vibration didn't feel completely hopeless and desolate like the lower vibrations I'd just experienced, but it was still deeply negative, violent and harmful. It was *anti-life*.

Again, the energy lifted me up higher. At the next level I felt doubt, worry, concern, stress and pessimism. This vibration, this *shade of grey*, was slightly lighter.

The next highest vibration was one of lethargy and stagnation. Here the vibration felt tired, drained, passive, complacent and discouraged. The emotions here weren't as negative as those at the lower levels, but they weren't positive either. The feeling here was of flatness. It was a dull place, a place of apathy, void of energy, vitality and colour. The life force here was that of a wilted flower, or a dying person.

When I was pulled up to the next vibration, something different occurred. I wasn't just lifted up, I was also pushed through a threshold.

It was as if I'd been raised up through a large grey cloud, like an aeroplane gaining altitude. Suddenly I found myself on the other side of the cloud in a vast blue expanse. Here, everything felt lighter and clearer. There was far more space compared with the lower vibrations, which had felt cramped and dark. Quite literally, I felt *uplifted*.

I realised then that I had transitioned from the darker to the lighter shades of grey. This vibration felt peaceful, contented, hopeful and happy. All around me was lightness and space.

Then once again, as soon as I'd understood the emotion of the place, I was moved upwards . . .

The next vibration I came to was of even more lightness. I was surrounded by a white light, and all around me I felt hope. This was a place of optimism, of deep peace and positivity. The positive emotions here were more potent than on the previous level, and they had more energy – more life force. There was more vibrancy here; more radiance and joy.

Then I started to travel up the light-grey spectrum more quickly. At each new vibration, I experienced more light, greater expanse and more life force. I experienced the emotions of enthusiasm and motivation, then inspiration and passion. Then there was wonder, exhilaration and joy, followed by radiance and splendour.

These higher vibrational states were so light-infused, so *ethereal,* that I was beginning to struggle to understand what they were. The feelings seemed to exist beyond the range of emotions we know on earth. They felt transcendental, cosmic, blissful beyond human comprehension. Yet somehow there was still more to experience.

Up again I travelled until I was brought to my final desti-nation, the highest level of the spectrum, which is the most difficult of all the levels to describe. No words can adequately convey what happened next; it's impossible to encompass the ecstasy that awaited me there. I had arrived at the place of pure positivity – the place of pure light. *Of light without any dark.*

When I arrived there, the light emanating from the vibra-tion was so strong that I was instantly blinded. The light didn't hurt my eyes, yet I couldn't see anything around me. It felt like millions of tiny needles of light were penetrating me, but I experienced no pain. Quite the opposite – it was as if countless little firecrackers of love and light were exploding inside me.

The light here was so pure that absolutely everything was illuminated. Nothing could escape the strength and reach of this light, and everything dark and hidden was transformed. The pervading sense was: *All will be illuminated.*

In that space I was being metamorphosed, alchemised by love and light. I was being fully held, understood and seen. I was experiencing deep, unconditional love.

The experience was ecstasy. It was an experience of pure bliss, joy, radiance and peace. This was pure love – the absolute euphoria of the sum total of all positive emotions. It was the highest denominator; the highest vibration on the spectrum: elation. This coming into the light was a homecoming, to myself, to my soul, to my spirit.

I had never felt so alive.
I had never felt so loved.
I had never felt so understood.
I had never felt so at home.
I had never felt so free.

For the first time since I was born, I was experiencing the bliss of my spirit-self. *I was home.*

I'm not sure how long I was in this space. It may have been ten minutes; it may have been more. But it felt like forever. It felt as though time was stretching out before me for eternity, and I was lost in the light.

I had travelled all the way up the spectrum from darkest dark to lightest light and now here I was, held in rapture. And yet, incredibly, that was only the start of what I was to experience that day. I was about to have my first encounter with time *beyond* the earth plane . . . I was about to experience circular time.

CHAPTER 16

THE CAVE

I understand that my experiences could seem as though they might be overwhelming. It took me months to process everything I'd witnessed and learned. I'm often asked if in their own spiritual work, others should expect or will need to go through something similar, and the answer is no. Each of us learns things – each of us is shown things – in a way that will be most accessible to us.

Psychics, intuitives, mystics and saints throughout the ages have often had these types of unique individual initiations which set them up for their life's work. I share what happened to me not to indicate that it is *the way* to understand one's soul purpose, but rather to relay that it was my way of learning it. Everyone travels a unique path, and while someone else may have similar experiences, it's likely that theirs will be different, at least in some ways.

I believe one of the reasons I was shown all these things was so that I could relay what I learned to others. As I will discuss later, the method I recommend (and practise myself) for attaining balance and insight is actually quite simple; it's a distillation of what I learned during these meditative experiences.

I had just travelled the entire vibrational spectrum from darkest dark to lightest light. What happened next was perhaps even more mind-blowing, partly because it happened *at the same time* as I had my vibrational experience.

Having multiple concurrent experiences is difficult for our rational minds to comprehend. Yet when you are in the midst of it, somehow it makes perfect sense. It is easy to feel and understand that the experiences are occurring in multiple dimensions, and that time is circular, not linear.

I was still resting in the highest vibration, experiencing the love and bliss of pure light, when another of my 'selves' began walking towards a door. There were now three of me: my first self, meditating in my white chair in my white office; my second self, standing and experiencing the vibration of pure light; and my third self, walking away from the vibration of pure light, towards a door. Some degree of my consciousness remained with each self, yet at this point my focus shifted primarily to the 'self' walking towards the door.

It was a large glass door with a turquoise handle. As I drew closer, I noticed it was covered with a beautiful gold-and-silver-patterned mosaic. A brilliant white light was shining from behind the door, illuminating the mosaic.

I reached out and opened the door. As I walked through it, I found myself standing on a path. Everything before me was misty and white, making it difficult to see too far ahead. I looked down at my feet; the marble stones beneath me were large and shiny and covered in the same gold and silver mosaic as the door.

I started walking. The path was long and sweeping, and it got quite windy at times; I kept having to change directions and reorientate myself to stay on track. Even so, as I walked along, I felt clear and hopeful and full of joy.

Suddenly, the path ended and I found myself standing outside a cave. It was large and brown, and jutted out from the earth. It reminded me of the large ant nests in the central desert of Australia, which are so tall and round you can mistake them for small boulders.

At the entranceway to the cave was a little door. It was dark, and I was apprehensive about trying to squeeze myself through it, yet I found myself moving forward anyway. Before I knew it, I was inside the cave.

It took a few moments for my eyes to adjust to the darkness, which painted the cave a deep indigo colour, like the rich blues and violets of the sky at nightfall. The vibration of the cave also felt darker than outside, almost *shadowy*, and my body tensed as I instinctively sensed that I was about to confront some of my deepest fears.

The room I was standing in was completely round, and I found myself in the very centre of it. There were drawings and lines etched in the dirt floor. They looked somewhat like compass points, but instead of the eight traditional directional markings, there were twelve. I bent down to take a closer look and saw that the directions were each marked by a small stone with a number painted in gold.

The line marked '1' was closest to me, just to the left of where I was standing. Without thinking, I walked over and stood upon it. As soon as I did, I found myself falling through the floor . . .

I land on my feet and as I look around, I see I'm standing in the middle of a large, square-shaped room. Though it's dark, I can make out the grey walls and the cobblestone floor. In front of me is a narrow spiral staircase lit by a few small torches that cast an eerie glow.

I'm overcome by the room's stifling energy. I search for a way out, but suddenly become aware that nothing bad could happen to me here, and that I've been sent here for an important reason. I begin to relax.

I look around and my eyes fall on an iron cage in the corner of the room. It's tall and narrow, and inside it is a woman. The cage is barely big enough to hold her. Her back is to me and she's sitting on the floor, facing the wall, her head in her hands. She's sobbing. Her long hair is matted and filthy, and she's wearing a dress that's been badly ripped. Most of her back is exposed, and I can see that it's covered with lash marks and bruises.

I take a step towards her and she quickly stands and turns to face me. Her eyes are wild and blue, her face pale and swollen, and there's a deep red gash running across her left cheek. I know somehow that she was once a beautiful woman, a woman of culture, class and nobility, but now she is a prisoner.

We lock eyes and immediately I understand — her soul is captured. Though she died many years before, she still believes she is trapped in this dungeon, in this place and time in history. She is an earthbound ghost.

'This woman is you in a past life,' my inner voice says to me. 'It is a fragment of your soul that is lost and stuck. You need to free both of you from her pain and put her soul to rest.' I walk towards the woman in the cage, my arms open and outstretched. When I reach her, I put both hands through the bars and touch her head. Then I look into her eyes. Words appear in my mind, then just as quickly come out of my mouth: 'I see your pain. I know your pain. I feel your pain. Let me help you heal your pain.'

The woman shudders and seems to relax. I repeat the words and again she shudders, then softens.

All at once, my head is filled with a story — her story. She had loved a married man and been imprisoned for adultery. She hadn't known he was married; she'd believed him when he told her he wasn't. But at the trial he had denounced her, calling her a liar, a seductress and a witch. She was sentenced to life imprisonment. This is why she's trapped in this dungeon — she has a broken heart, and a broken belief in truth and love.

I say the words to her again. In a flash, a powerful white light floods the room, drenching us in its magnificent glow.

Before my eyes, the woman begins to transform. It starts at the top of her head — her dirty and matted hair untangles and becomes clean and shiny and blonde. Then all the bruises and the gash across her face disappear, and the colour returns to her cheeks. Her bodice is suddenly mended; her white satin skirts are crisp and clean. Finally, her pearls and jewels are made sparkling and beautiful.

The woman now stands tall, beautiful and regal; her pain and suffering is gone. The cage door opens and she walks out.

In a flash she transforms again, this time morphing into a bright ball of light. The ball spins and hovers over me momentarily, then shoots upwards, out of the dungeon.

I stand there in awe, knowing that now she is free. We are free. A fragment of my soul has just returned to me.

Suddenly the dungeon dematerialises and I'm back in the cave, standing on the line of the number 1. Automatically, I walk over to the line marked '2'. As soon as I do, I'm falling through the floor again . . .

I land, and this time I'm not in a dungeon, but a tower of sorts. Somehow I've 'moved up' into this tower, which is high and round, with walls made of pale-coloured stone and large round windows that overlook fields of green and brown.

The air feels old and trapped; the room reeks of death. To my right is a large wooden door, and when I turn to look at it, I see her — a woman in chains. Her dress is dirty and ripped, and she's crouched down, crying, her hands covering her face.

She is painfully thin, and her arms and legs are covered in black bruises and welts. Her dark hair has been roughly shaved – there are patches of blood and scabs on her scalp.

She, too, is trapped in her despair. I walk towards her, saying the words I know will free her. 'I see your pain. I feel your pain. I know your pain. Let me help you heal your pain.' Instantly, she stops crying and looks up at me. There is hope in her eyes, among all her terror and fear. I reach out and touch her on the head and say the words again, and in that moment, I receive a flash of her tragedy.

This woman is a psychic and healer who had been captured and tortured. She was once a respected woman, but is now a 'witch' and 'heretic'. Many of the people in the village who had benefited from her knowledge and predictions had denounced her. She's awaiting her death.

When I say the words, white light begins to beam down onto both of us. I watch as her dark hair grows back long and full, her face is healed of its bruises and scars and her dress is cleaned and repaired. The chains and bindings fall from her wrists and ankles . . . When the transformation is complete, before me stands a magnificent, powerful woman with raven hair and glistening eyes.

Then, as with the woman in the dungeon, her form dissolves into a ball of light. It shoots upwards, out of the tower. She transitions, and I'm returned again to the cave.

As I made my way through lines 3 to 7, I discovered that some of these past lives – those containing my soul fragments – were ancient, dating back to prehistory. None of them matched the past-life recollections that had come to me when I'd first moved to Germany, though many had the same recurring themes: being persecuted for seeing and telling the truth, and for having psychic and intuitive abilities. But there were other themes as well.

On line 8, I encountered a teenage girl unable to fulfil her dreams as a performer because she was afflicted with an illness. She had been a talented dancer and singer, but was crippled by a strange sickness that damaged her legs. When I freed that teenage girl, the part of my soul that was a *repressed performer* was also freed.

On line 9, I saw an elderly gentleman dressed in his night-robe, hunched over a desk and scribbling furiously. I saw that he'd written a series of revolutionary books, which he'd been tortured and imprisoned for. All the books, his entire life's work, had been burned or destroyed, and now he was desperately trying to rewrite them. When I freed him, I released a *repressed author and visionary* portion of myself.

On line 10, I was in a temple – a huge, cathedral-like building with massive stained-glass windows and hundreds of white marble pews. There was a teacher – a priestess of sorts, wearing a long white robe and gold headdress. When everyone fell silent, she tried to speak, but no sound came. She'd lost the power of speech. Speaking and lecturing was her life's passion, and she was devastated that she could no longer conduct her services. She felt like a charlatan, too, because she didn't know what was wrong with her or how she could heal it. In this soul retrieval, I saw that I had been a *repressed teacher and healer*.

On line 11, I saw a painter, a young boy of eleven. This child had painted canvases of immense proportions – magnificent, majestic paintings of angels and saints – but I found him sitting with his head bowed, despondent, in a room full of half-finished canvases. He was grieving because his mother had forbidden him to paint. Fearful of his prodigious talent, she had given away his brushes and paints and sent him to a monastery. The pain of not being able to paint was so great that within the year, he hanged himself from a tree. In this soul retrieval, I freed my *repressed artist* from his pain and anguish.

In each of these eleven experiences, I had identified and retrieved a piece of my soul that, having been imprisoned, was still affecting me in this lifetime. These had kept me from living my soul purpose. When I stepped on the line marked '12', a different experience awaited me.

CHAPTER 17

FROM DARK TO LIGHT

At each of the previous numbers, I had encountered a single, tangible past life where a piece of my soul had been trapped. When I stepped onto line 12, I felt myself being swept upwards; it was like I was flying straight up into the sky.

I landed on what initially seemed to be the peak of a mountain, but as my senses adjusted, I realised that what I was standing on was the highest point of some kind of glass dome. I looked down at my feet and saw that the glass was emitting a brilliant white light: the *pure light*. The energy emanating from it was amazing, and I was overtaken by euphoria.

I noticed a group of tall, slender beings dressed in long white robes walking towards me. They had long, straight white hair and beautiful faces with large, pale-blue eyes the colour of glacial lakes. There were about twenty or so of these beings, and I wasn't sure if they were male or female – they seemed to be both.

These angels looked at me lovingly as they formed a circle around me. I saw that their robes were tied with either a gold, violet or turquoise sash, as though to indicate a sort of hierarchy among them. As they closed the circle, I was asked telepathically to move to the centre of it.

As soon as I did, a sensation like a wave engulfed me, lifting me up and propelling me, as if I was riding the crest of the wave. Back it took me, through time and space until, just as suddenly, I was once again standing still. The wave had taken me back in time to my very first incarnation on earth.

I saw that I'd been born a male child and had lived only a few weeks due to a heart condition. This life wasn't influential or eventful, but it was my soul's *very first* incarnation.

As soon as I'd seen and understood this, the wave moved me once more, to my second incarnation on earth. Again, I was born a male child, and had lived that life as a slave who died from heat stroke.

One by one, I was taken through all my past lives. My past-life history had spanned thousands of years and I'd chosen to incarnate hundreds and hundreds of times – many times on earth, but also on planets in other galaxies. Between incarnations, I would return to my life on the Other Side. There I would rest and resume my life, and when I was ready, I would begin to plan my next incarnation.

Many souls, including myself, were eager to incarnate into another life because this granted us the opportunity to deepen our experience of love. On the Other Side we know

ourselves to be 'one with all that is', b.
of our true home and entering into the a.
plane (or other places with lower vibrations),
ence greater love. Experiencing polarity – light an.
and fear – which doesn't exist in our true home, ena
to arrive at higher insights and understandings. *We can o.*
truly know ourselves to be the light when we are confronted with
the dark.

Through this experience, I also learned that the ultimate spiritual goal is to rediscover that you are love and light and one with the entire universe while you are away from your soul home. In other words, our primary goal in coming to earth is to awaken to our own divine inner light here, among the fear and darkness around us.

As I experienced my past lives, I also discovered that although each soul creates a life-map, planning out its next incarnation, there is no guarantee that these goals and visions will be fulfilled. The Law of Free Will operates on the earth plane, meaning that once a soul enters the womb and then is born, anything can happen. That's why, when I worked briefly as a fortune-teller, it was impossible for me to tell people their futures – because they are not set in stone. Our choices matter; what we do in life shapes our path.

Once I saw and understood all these things, the wave transported me one last time, and I saw myself being born into this lifetime. I saw myself inside my mother's womb; I saw my vibrations lowering so that I could adjust to the earth plane; I saw myself being born and I saw how the silver cord attaching me to my soul home on the Other Side was cut.

atched my incarnation as Belinda, I saw myself falling
into the vibration of the earth plane, my once-radiant,
light-filled self quickly becoming fearful and dark. The moment
my cord was cut, I was born, and I took my first breath as Belinda.

I then saw everything that had taken place in my life –
every experience, every decision, every realisation up until this
point, these moments in August 2007, when I was sitting in
my white chair in my white office meditating. I saw everything
about my life in painstaking detail.

Some of the things I saw, I can't explain – they are too
complex to put into words. But I saw many things that I had
mapped out before I came to earth, such as being my Grandma
Jean's granddaughter and being my mother's daughter. I also
saw that I had planned to incarnate into Australia and then
return to Europe early in my lifetime, and that I'd chosen to
be born with red hair and green eyes – the traditional Celtic
markings of a witch.

I also saw that I had planned to be born too psychic.
I actually wanted to have scary and unsettling experiences with
people's negative emotions, sicknesses, ghosts, the church and
the shadow aspects of the psychic and spirit realms, because
I knew these experiences would help me acquire certain skills
that would help me fulfil my soul purpose.

I saw that I would use these spiritual gifts to help people
heal themselves and find their way back to the light. I discovered that I had chosen to experience as much of the dark as
possible, so I could show others how to heal their shadows
and rise up. I'd chosen to know the dark of my gifts because it
would enable me to help others.

During this experience, I also came to understand what soul purpose really means – it consists of those things that we love best and do best. I was shown that our soul purpose is the *fusion of our talents and passions*, and that when we are living these out and expressing them, we are on fire with life. In this state we are powerful, luminous and strong, and from this place we become spiritual change agents, spreading beauty and light wherever we go.

By embracing our talents and passions, we can heal our shadow and embrace our light. This is our *collective* soul purpose – to heal ourselves so we can *heal the world*.

As suddenly as the whole experience had begun, it ended. I opened my eyes and found myself back in my white office, sitting in my white chair. In earth time, just one hour had passed.

CHAPTER 18

REVELATIONS

The days following my enlightened moment were spent in meditation and resting, recuperating and writing down everything I'd experienced. I knew something profound had happened – the universe had revealed its secrets to me – but I was also perplexed by it.

As grateful as I was for these experiences, I couldn't stop wondering how this had happened to me. How had I travelled the spectrum from dark to light? How had I retrieved my soul fragments? How had I come to know these things about my soul and my soul purpose, and the journey that all souls take?

Was it just spontaneous – a once-in-a-lifetime experience? Or could it be brought about or triggered somehow? I wanted to be able to consciously access these vibrations and dimensions, to journey there again and understand more. And most importantly, I wanted other people to know and experience what had been revealed to me. But how?

I didn't need to wait long for the answer.

Three days after that meditation, I was again sitting in my office, meditating and practising presence, when I suddenly found myself being pulled upwards into the high, blissful vibration of pure light.

Again, I was immediately engulfed by feelings of love and lightness and, again, I was looking at myself from outside. There were two of me, and I somehow knew I was about to witness something powerful and marvellous.

Suddenly a white light appeared from above me – the beautiful, exquisite *pure light* from before. I saw a large, round, luminous column of pure light stream down from the heavens. The light was coming towards me, then it was pouring down from the heavens into my body. The feeling was incredible.

In that moment, watching the pure light streaming into me, I saw my real self; my true, essential and light-filled self. I saw my full energy field and my chakras.

My energy field was a vast field of light, radiant and magnificently designed. Within the field were twelve chakras – twelve powerful centres that looked like vortexes or spinning wheels of light.

I saw that seven of my chakras – my lower ones – were located within my body and head, and five of my chakras – the higher ones – were located above my head. My highest chakra, my chakra 12, was receiving the pure light and acting as a sort of funnel for it, pushing it into my lower chakras, all the way down to chakra 1 and into the earth.

Pure light was streaming into me, and I was *embodying* heaven on earth.

In that moment, I learned something else of great importance: that the chakras play a crucial role in my life. As I looked upon my energy field and the pure light streaming into my chakras, I saw that each chakra had a different geometric and energetic structure. Each chakra was designed slightly differently, and each has a unique purpose, with the job of looking after individual aspects of my life.

I then realised something of monumental importance, which has become the foundation of my entire life's work: *if certain areas of our lives aren't working properly, it's because our chakras aren't working properly!*

I also saw that the chakras not only fulfil their own unique purpose and destiny, but also work together to serve our soul purpose. If we can't discover and live our purpose, it's because our chakras aren't working properly.

The chakras are essential to our soul purpose.

As the pure light streamed into me, I saw that the problems in my life – bad health, exhaustion, money issues – were the result of blockages in my chakras, and that these blockages manifested themselves as patches of grey and black, or rips, tears, distortions or stagnations in my energy.

I understood that blockages cause the chakras to work sluggishly or otherwise improperly. They cause negative and self-depleting belief systems, which in turn cause negative and self-sabotaging life experiences.

Witnessing this led to a further revelation: that there is a difference between the lower and higher chakras. I saw that my seven lower chakras look after my present life – my health, my relationships, my career, my creativity, and so on – while my five higher chakras look after my soul – my talents, passions and spiritual gifts. I realised that until we heal our lower chakras, we can't effectively access our higher ones.

But this was not all I was to experience . . .

As the pure light continued to stream into my energy field, coming into me through my higher chakras, I felt myself being lifted up. Just like in my previous experience, another 'me' appeared.

There was the me that was sitting in my office having the pure light pour into my energy field. There was the me observing this taking place, understanding and assimilating all that was being revealed about the chakras and healing. And now, again, there was another me; a third me that was being lifted up higher and higher, into another vibration and dimension.

When this third me came to rest, I found myself standing in front of the same large glass door from a few days before.

Again, there was the beautiful gold-and-silver-patterned mosaic and the brilliant light shining from behind it. As I went to open the door, with striking clarity and illumination I suddenly knew: The journey into the five higher cosmic chakras is the path to discovering your true soul purpose. *But first you need to work on your lower seven chakras and heal your shadow.*

And with that, the meditation ended, and my life was changed forever.

CHAPTER 19

GETTING STARTED

I now refer to the experiences and revelations I had during those meditations as my 'enlightened moment'. In those remarkable sessions, not only had I healed my own past-life wounds, changed my energy and discovered my soul purpose, I had also been shown how to help others do the same.

Since my enlightened moment, I have worked with my chakras every single day. And I can attest that each of those revelations has held true. Since then, I've helped thousands of people apply what I learned, and it has transformed their lives just as it did mine.

When your energy shifts as much and as quickly as mine did during those days in August 2007, your life is turned upside down and inside out. Within only a few months, my relationship ended and I moved back to Australia. My friends and clients in Germany fell away, and all that was left from my old life were the belongings I took back to Australia with me. It was as if my entire life before that moment had simply dissolved.

This wasn't an easy time; it required a lot of faith. But I knew I'd had a huge shift and that my life just needed to vibrationally catch up. And I trusted I was being led to much higher shores, which of course I was.

During this time of huge shifting and change, the chakra work became like a friend to me – a steady companion. I developed my Chakra Cleanse Meditation, and every day I would sit in silence, meditating and working on my energy field and chakras. This practice lovingly held me and healed me.

We often want things to come quickly, but patience is an important tool – one enabled by the practice of presence. I gave myself time to just sit and be, to assimilate all my new insights and knowledge.

In that time, my lifelong stomach and digestive problems were healed. My oversensitive and empath nature came into balance; I no longer energetically took on others' pain and negativity. My panic disorder disappeared, and the headaches and constant back pain that had plagued me were resolved. And I no longer felt burdened by my psychic gifts and abilities.

Working on my chakras also gave me much more energy and drive. I was used to feeling lethargic, drained and dragging, but suddenly I felt clear and invigorated. It also healed my self-worth issues, and I grew much more confident and outgoing. Instead of wanting to change myself, I started to embrace those things that were uniquely me, and as a result I began to surround myself with people who were lifting me up instead of pulling me down.

I also became much more prosperous, and could easily attract money into my life, as well as support and care. I grew much more self-empowered, and learned to know and speak out about what I did and didn't want.

Thanks to my new connection with myself, I knew I no longer wanted to work strictly as a medical intuitive. Over the course of many years I began to work more as a writer, speaker and mentor. During this time I met my husband and soulmate, Pete, and in 2009 we had a daughter.

I also created an online business in 2012 where I regularly write articles and offer free spiritual support. Tens of thousands of people subscribe to my newsletter.

During those intervening years, when I still worked one on one as a medical intuitive, I shared with my clients what I'd learned from my experiences. I showed them how to heal their lives by cleansing and balancing their chakras.

I started to include a chakra diagnosis in my sessions. Once I knew how important the chakras were, I made them a major focus of my work. Over the years, I've consistently watched chakra balancing and cleansing transform people's lives.

I've watched my clients quickly heal their health problems. I've seen them quit jobs they no longer wanted and easily manifest new ones. They've been able to heal their marriages and family hurts, and overcome insecurities and self-doubt. They discovered their passion and soul purpose, and bravely began to live the life of their dreams. I've witnessed huge breakthroughs, and seen people transition to a much *higher* life.

And now it's time to help you do the same.

PART 2

CHANGE YOUR CHAKRAS, CHANGE YOUR LIFE

CHAPTER 20

THE CHAKRAS

In the 'how to' portion of this book, I will explain how I took my experiences and translated them into a set of practices that thousands of people have now used to heal their energy systems.

In today's world of noise and uncertainty, we need practices that keep our chakras strong, healthy and secure. We must be luminous and light-filled, connected to the vibration of pure light, while remaining grounded. These practices will help you achieve this.

The core of these practices lies in balancing your chakras. A good understanding of the chakras and how they work is helpful to 'diagnosing' any problems you're having in your energy anatomy. So in the chapters to come, I will:

❖ discuss each of the chakras and the areas they govern, and how imbalances or blockages in a specific chakra could impact your life;

❖ show you how you can self-assess your chakras and outline exercises to nourish each of your chakras; and

❖ delve into the Chakra Cleansing Meditation that will help you to balance your chakra system.

There is a lot of information out there about the chakras that describes these centres or wheels of light in our bodies. Some texts go back centuries. The chakra system has deep roots in Hinduism, and has been observed by humans for hundreds of years. I have chosen not to discuss other writings here, because the truth is that I haven't read many of them. My understanding of the chakras and how they work, along with the methods I'll discuss for strengthening and supporting them, comes from my own direct experience as a medical intuitive and through working with my own chakras.

Through my work, along with my own meditative practices, I've grown to understand more deeply what the chakras are, how they function and how we can best support them. In this book I only describe the practices that I know will help you balance and strengthen your chakras.

Your chakras

Within you is a complete and highly intelligent energy system that governs your entire life. It is comprised of twelve chakras, which are energy vortexes that govern specific areas of your life, ranging from your physical and emotional wellbeing to your spiritual health. These energy centres make up your energy field, and your energy field and chakras together make up your energy anatomy.

Put simply, the state of your chakras and energy field determines the state of your life – your health, wealth, love life, career, success and joy. Your inner world creates your outer world. Get your chakras working and your life will follow!

Seven of your twelve chakras have their focal point in your physical body; the other five exist above your physical body. (Technically, chakra 7 exists above the body, but the focal point for working with it is the top of the head.) Together, the chakras create a large and luminous field of light.

Each of these chakras fuels and sustains certain aspects of your life. They do this by receiving energy from the universe and then transporting this energy to the areas of your life and physical body where they are focused.

In this way, your chakras look after every aspect of your life and health. You have a chakra that looks after your creativity, and one that is responsible for creating abundance. You have a chakra dedicated to making your life joyful and fun, one that is responsible for helping you discover your soul purpose, and so on.

Here is a brief overview of the individual functions of each chakra:

❖ Chakra 1 grounds you and helps you feel connected to your body and the earth plane.
❖ Chakra 2 helps you attract into your life that which you desire.

- ❖ Chakra 3 makes sure you forge your own path and protects you and your energy.
- ❖ Chakra 4 connects you with your heart and teaches you love and compassion.
- ❖ Chakra 5 reveals to you your own individuality and uniqueness.
- ❖ Chakra 6 opens you up to your spiritual and mystical gifts and talents.
- ❖ Chakra 7 shows you the true nature of the cosmos: unconditional love.
- ❖ Chakras 8–12 help you discover your true soul purpose.

While your twelve chakras each have individual tasks, they also function as a whole, with each chakra influencing and working together with the others. In this way, the health and functionality of each chakra affects the health and functionality of all your chakras. For example, a weak chakra 1 can block the flow of energy to chakra 2.

When your chakras receive energy from the universe, they either pull the energy up from the ground (the earth-to-heaven energy flow system), or they pull it down from the heavens (the heaven-to-earth energy flow system). When your energy field pulls energy up from the earth, it starts by pulling it into chakra 1. The energy then moves its way up to chakra 2, and so on until it reaches chakra 12. Similarly, when you receive energy from the heavens, this energy-flow current travels down from chakra 12, into chakra 11, and all the way down to chakra 1.

If there are blockages in *any* of the chakras – if they aren't working properly – your energy-flow current will be compromised. And if your energy flow is compromised, you'll experience recurring problems, which will stop you from having an amazing life!

To be clear, while the lower chakras carry a *lower vibration* than the higher ones, this doesn't mean they are in any way *negative*. The lower chakras are simply more embodied, more *earthly* – they govern what is more to do with this earth plane than the higher chakras. Each chakra, whether lower or higher, is beautiful and powerful and equally important in supporting you.

Why chakras don't work properly

Your chakras are funnels for energy, as well as energy generators and distributors. If their ability to receive, generate and distribute energy is compromised, they can't do their jobs properly.

Think of the chakras as eager, diligent workers. If they are tired, unwell and underfed, they can't work productively; if they can't work productively, they become blocked, stagnant and weak.

But how do our chakras become weak or blocked in the first place? By the pain and shadow we take on when we incarnate on earth. Each time we return here, we also return to the negative conditionings of our past lives. And throughout life, we pick up on and absorb the negative subconscious beliefs of others. All of this *taints* our chakras.

Think about it: You are who you are and you believe what you do about life due to many different influences. These include your country of birth, your culture, your race, your language, how you were raised, the genes you inherited from your parents, your parents' personalities, where you spent your childhood, where you went to school, who your first best friend was, and so on.

There are also other, more esoteric influences. The placement of the moon, the sun and the planets at the time of your birth; your mother's experience during your birth; your experience in the womb; your past lives; your life on the Other Side, and so on. These all have a bearing on our attitudes and beliefs.

In other words, you are the sum total of many beliefs and opinions about life, as well as a variety of circumstances over which you have no control. You didn't consciously choose most of these things, and some of them you didn't even directly experience! Yet they all have the effect of weakening your chakras.

To heal ourselves and our lives, we need to counteract the negative influences that are working on us and our chakras. We need to change our belief systems from negative life-depleting ones to positive life-affirming ones.

But this requires something other than repeating positive affirmations or mantras. Doing these things can be powerful, but I call it 'taking the long way around'. The problems in our lives are there because of the problems in our energy systems. That's why changing our thoughts has limited impact. But when we heal our energy systems, a new, more positive way of thinking naturally emerges, and our life circumstances change (not the other way around).

It's important to note that changing your chakras does not replace the need to seek medical help. When you heal your chakras, you draw into your life those people who help you and support you, not only with your health but with all areas of your life. I believe it is important to take a holistic approach to health, working together with both doctors of medicine and alternative healthcare practitioners.

Before we talk about *how* to work with your chakras to change your energy and change your life, let's look at each of the chakras and the aspects of your life that they govern. Chapters 21 to 27 explore the seven earthly chakras and give you the resources to self-assess your chakras, as well as exercises, hobbies and activities to help you heal each individual chakra.

CHAPTER 21

CHAKRA 1: GROUNDING

Chakra 1 is the first level of your energy anatomy. It's also called the root chakra or base chakra, not only because of its location (at the perineum and between the feet), but also because chakra 1 is the beginning of our journey here on earth, and is the chakra that 'roots' and 'grounds' us.

At your essence, you are a *spiritual being without form*. All of us exist as spirits on the Other Side until we choose to incarnate again. When we return to earth and take on an earthly body, we lower our vibration to accommodate the lower vibration on earth (as compared to the very high vibration of the Other Side). As you grew in the womb and were then born, you slowly began to adjust to the physical world of matter and form. To protect your new physical body, you need basic survival instincts. You also need to accept earth as your home away from home for the duration of your stay here. Chakra 1 oversees these instincts.

You can think of chakra 1 as your energetic foundation; it governs your survival needs, driving you to obtain what you need to exist here in physical form. If your first chakra is functioning properly, you seek out food, water and shelter, and will defend your body – as well as the things necessary to your survival – if they are threatened. If your first chakra is balanced, you can readily manifest that which you *need* to survive this journey on earth.

To live a healthy life, your physical body also needs stamina and strength. A balanced first chakra provides these, and helps you connect with and draw energy from the earth and nature. This link helps you feel supported, nourished and cared for.

Just as humans are designed to connect with nature, we are also designed to connect with one another. We are 'herd animals' – being part of a group or tribe helps us to survive and thrive. Therefore, chakra 1 also oversees your drive to seek out a tribe – a community to which you belong, and feel loved and accepted by. A sense of connection is essential to developing healthy self-esteem; without this, life is full of struggle.

A feeling of disconnection from your surroundings can also cause you to struggle; you need to be where you can thrive. Your first chakra drives you to find that place or environment in the world in which you are truly 'at home'. If chakra 1 is balanced, you will not only feel loved and accepted in your family and community, but you'll also love the place where you live.

Chakra 1 basics

Names
This chakra is also called the first chakra, base chakra or root chakra.

Location
Chakra 1 is the only chakra for which there are two points – the perineum *and* between the feet.

Areas of body governed
This chakra oversees the physical areas of the spinal column, legs, feet, hips and the lower part of the large intestine (colon).

Drive and issues
Chakra 1 governs our drive to survive, as well as to seek out a tribe and environment in which we feel at home. This is the chakra that grounds us and gives us a sense of belonging in the world.

Let's look at some clients I've worked with and see how a chakra 1 imbalance affected their lives. Then we'll explore this chakra in more detail.

Note: In my twenty years of working as a medical intuitive, I gave hundreds of sessions, conducting them all in the same way I described in Chapter 14. After my enlightened moment, I added a chakra diagnosis, which I would do after reading their past lives.

Most case studies presented in this book are from individual client sessions. In a few cases, I have combined pieces from several different clients to present a broader view of different issues that can occur when the chakras are out of balance. In all cases, names have been changed to protect clients' identities.

Case studies

Pauline

Pauline is at the end of her rope. She arrives several minutes late for her session looking exhausted; she's got dark circles under her eyes, her skin is pale, and when she takes a seat, she shrinks into the armchair.

Though the session hasn't even started, right away I can see that Pauline is in her mid-thirties and has been diagnosed with chronic fatigue syndrome. For the last eight years, she has 'tried everything', but nothing seems to help. She also suffers from chronic lower back pain, constipation and iron deficiency.

After I tell Pauline how the session will run, I tell her my initial impressions. 'Yes, that's correct, but I don't know what to do,' she says, nearly in tears. 'And then there's my love life.'

'Your relationships often end up in co-dependent or otherwise in unhappy spaces,' I say as impressions keep coming to me.

'That's right,' she sighs. 'Part of the problem is I just never feel good.'

When I ask Pauline about her living situation, she says she rents a place in a noisy building in the city. It's difficult for her to sleep well at night because of the sounds from the street and adjacent apartments. She says she'd love to live out in the country, or at least go there on weekends, but she can never seem to get moving.

I scan Pauline's energy as she's talking, and I'm not surprised to see that her first chakra is severely weakened. 'Your base chakra is in such an underactive state that it's incapable of drawing up energy,' I tell her. 'And when your first chakra can't draw up energy, your body and your entire energy field become depleted.' I explain that although the two don't always go hand in hand, I've seen many people with a diagnosis of chronic fatigue who also have a very weak first chakra.

'But there's hope. If you work with your first chakra to strengthen it, this should significantly improve your physical symptoms, along with the rest of your life.'

'Really?' she asks. It's the first spark of life I've seen in her all session.

'Absolutely,' I say. I encourage her to follow her desire to spend more time in the country. 'Your connection with the earth and nature is a critical component of supporting your first chakra. That's why you're getting that urge to get out of town. Follow it!'

David

'I'm trying not to move around anymore,' David tells me, 'but it's just not happening.' David is in his early fifties

151

and for most of his life, he's felt the need to move house every eighteen months or so. As I listen to him, I see images of homes in Italy, Sweden, Germany, Canada, Holland, England and New Zealand. The worn leather shoulder bag at his feet clearly has some miles on it, and as I watch David in the chair across from me, even now he's having trouble sitting still.

'It's been an adventure,' he tells me, 'but by my late thirties, I got tired of moving all the time. The trouble is, I just can't stop. It's gotten exhausting, and the expense of so much moving has badly impacted my financial situation.'

'Yes, my attention is pulled to your first chakra. Every time you try to settle down, something happens. Either your work sends you away again, you can't tolerate your disruptive neighbours, the apartment just isn't right, the relationship ends or something else goes wrong.'

'Yes!' David says. 'I don't know what to do. I just want to settle down and stay put.'

'Do you really?' I ask.

'What do you mean?' he responds, eyebrows raised.

'Well, your first chakra is showing me that you equate "settling down" with boredom and a loss of youth and fun. You believe that if you stop moving, your life will end. The fun will stop and you'll be confined.'

David goes to say something, then closes his mouth. He sits back and rubs his moustache. 'My first instinct was to say that's not true,' he says, 'that you're wrong. But you know, now that I think about it, my father feels this way. I think it's something I inherited from him.

CHAKRA 1
Red, base chakra, root chakra

Governs
Spinal column, legs,
feet, hips, lower part
of the large intestine
(colon)

Drive
To ensure one's survival
and make sure we have
everything we need
here on earth

Issues
Grounding,
survival, belonging,
the body

Likes
Red, nature, grounding
(walking, hiking,
gardening), all forms
of movement including
exercise, environments
in which you feel good
and at home

CHAKRA 2
Orange, sacral chakra

Governs
Lower abdomen, pelvis, reproductive system, kidneys, bladder, upper part of the large intestine (colon)

Drive
Pursuit of individuation and pleasure

Issues
Individuation, magnetism, sexuality, pleasure, creative expression

Likes
Orange, beautiful environments (art galleries, botanical gardens, old Gothic churches), massages, hugs, lovemaking, romance, sunsets, losing yourself in the present moment, dancing naked, anything you find delightful

CHAKRA 3
Yellow, solar plexus chakra

Governs
Stomach, liver, gallbladder, digestive system, spleen

Drive
Personal power and boundaries

Issues
Self-esteem, self-empowerment, will, ambition

Likes
Yellow, saying 'no' if something isn't right for you, martial arts, holding your centre when confronted, knowing your truth, focus, persistence, diligence, diplomacy, strength of character, being a 'peaceful warrior'

CHAKRA 4
Green, heart chakra

Governs
Heart, blood, chest, hands and arms, lungs, circulatory system

Drive
Pursuit and expression of love

Issues
Self-love, giving and receiving love, compassion, forgiveness and acceptance

Likes
Green, anything heartfelt (hugs, talks, movies), smiles, kind words, forgiveness, letting go of old hurts, visualising people living in health and harmony, telling others how much you love them, random acts of kindness, undertaking activities you love

CHAKRA 5
Blue, throat chakra

Governs
Throat, neck, jaw,
teeth, thyroid glands,
vocal cords

Drive
Authentic and
original expression,
self-determination and
will, speaking one's truth

Issues
Ability to express
needs and desires,
open and honest
communication,
creativity, surrendering
personal will to
divine will

Likes
Blue, singing, public
speaking, writing, acting,
performing, speaking your
truth, interesting discussions
with like-minded people,
any activity in which you
express yourself

CHAKRA 6
Indigo, third eye chakra

Governs
Head, brain
(hypothalamus, pituitary
gland, pituitary nerve
plexus), ears, eyes

Drive
Transcendence
(to go 'above
and beyond')

Issues
Wisdom (the balance
of imagination and
intellect), intuition
and clairvoyance,
creating our
own reality

Likes
Indigo, meditation,
visualisation, brainstorming
and goal setting, consciously
dreaming your perfect life,
any activity that inspires
you to stretch yourself
and be great

CHAKRA 7
Violet, crown chakra

Governs
Upper brain and
nervous system

Drive
Oneness, surrendering
to divinity

Issues
Enlightenment
and soul purpose

Likes
Violet, meditation,
stillness and reflection,
books about saints, yogis,
and great men and
women of the world

CHAKRAS 8–12
Cosmic chakras or soul purpose chakras

Governs
Soul purpose

Drive
Knowing yourself
to be a cosmic
being of light

Issues
Discovering
your true
soul purpose

Likes
Pure light

'When we were kids, my sisters and I were moved around all the time — every eighteen months to two years, in fact. Dad would get restless and he'd sell the house and build or buy another one. We were always "in transit". He'd say to us that we need to get out and live life and keep moving; otherwise, our lives would be over.'

David sits quietly for another minute, then shakes his head and offers a wry smile. 'I can see now that my dad's behaviour and beliefs have affected my life. What can I do to stop it, though?'

'We've got to get your first chakra working properly,' I tell him. 'It's the job of your base chakra to help you find your true "home" in the world. When you do this, your life will work and you'll find both your metaphoric and real-world homes.'

Katja

I'm speaking to Katja on the phone, and the first thing I notice is her lacklustre tone. It sounds flat and lifeless, as if she's watching her life go by instead of living it.

When I begin to scan her energy field, I find that it too is lacking lustre. Most of her chakras are washed out and pale, and I receive the image of her being like a wilting plant that isn't getting enough water and sunshine. Unfortunately, many of Katja's chakras are weak and blocked, her first chakra particularly so.

'Katja,' I say, 'I see that you're struggling to make ends meet. You're feeling lonely, living on welfare and estranged from your only daughter.'

'Yes,' Katja says without a trace of emotion or self-pity. 'Everything you've said is true. I'm poor and alone.'

I see no fire in Katja's energy field – no sense of engagement in life. What I do see in her first chakra is that most of the time she feels 'out of it'.

'Your energy is very ungrounded,' I say.

'I'm not surprised,' she says. 'All my life I felt sort of dizzy; not quite here. Most of the time I find myself mentally drifting away.' She tells me she's also constantly fatigued and has lived with depression for as long as she can remember.

There's something else I can see in Katja's first chakra. In a past life she was accused of stealing money from a rich family and sent to prison, then hanged. She hadn't committed the crime, and had proclaimed her innocence even while being tortured, but she was convicted anyway. The trauma and betrayal in this past life was causing Katja to fear being back on earth again.

'Katja,' I say, 'do you think of this earth plane as a dark and cruel place?'

She shudders and whispers, 'Yes, I don't like it here at all.' I tell Katja that she's being affected by a past-life memory. 'These memories run deep within us, especially those in which we have experienced trauma. Even if we can't consciously remember them,' I say, 'they still exist in our chakras, where they can hinder the flow of energy throughout our energy field. That's why cleansing and looking after our chakras is so important. Otherwise we can still be living out past-life struggles, as you are. I can help you clear this from your first chakra, and if you commit

154

to a regular meditation practice, I'm confident things will improve for you.'

'Well, I'm willing to try it,' Katja says, though I still don't hear any real conviction in her voice. For her sake, I hope she will.

These examples show some of the many issues and challenges that can stem from a weak or imbalanced chakra 1. Let's look at your first chakra and see how fit and healthy it is.

Chakra 1 self-assessment

To get an idea of how fit and healthy your first chakra is, ask yourself the following questions:

Y / N Am I grounded in my physical body and in my life?

Y / N Do I have and seek out a connection to nature?

Y / N Do I look after my physical body through a good diet, relaxation, adequate rest and exercise?

Y / N Do I feel that I belong to a community or tribe?

Y / N Do I live in an environment I love, where I feel safe, secure and at home?

Y / N Can I easily manifest and create what I need to live in this world?

Y / N Am I free of problems with my lower spine, legs, feet, hips and/or large intestine?

If you answered 'no' to one or two of these questions, you have some challenges with your first chakra. If you answered 'no' to many of them, you probably have a significant blockage.

Chakra 1 out of balance

If your first chakra is not working properly, you may have challenges with your physical or emotional health, finances, love life, relationships with family and friends, or your career and creativity, such as the following:

Physical health

- ❖ Weakness or other issues in your legs (such as varicose veins), hips, back or knees
- ❖ Lower back pain, sciatica
- ❖ Chronic constipation or sluggish bowel
- ❖ Chronic fatigue
- ❖ Iron deficiency
- ❖ Some autoimmune diseases or low immunity
- ❖ Being overweight or obese
- ❖ Feeling disconnected from your body

Emotional health

- ❖ Feeling scattered, forgetful or tired
- ❖ Feeling ungrounded, dizzy or floaty
- ❖ Stuck in a struggle cycle, which causes a feeling of burnout
- ❖ Wanting to 'check out', frequently wishing you were someplace else
- ❖ Attracting dramas that create more drama and stress
- ❖ Feeling lazy, fatigued or depressed
- ❖ Feeling chronically tired and stressed

Finances

- ❖ Stuck in poverty or a struggle cycle
- ❖ Living from pay cheque to pay cheque
- ❖ Struggling with greed and hoarding
- ❖ Overly focused on material possessions

Love life

- ❖ Driven by the need to feel secure
- ❖ Inability to feel safe and secure and trust yourself, others and life
- ❖ Don't have time for a relationship
- ❖ Low libido

Relationships with friends and family

- ❖ Driven by the need to feel secure
- ❖ Inability to feel safe and secure and trust yourself, others and life
- ❖ Inability to feel settled and connected to home and your family members
- ❖ Inability to provide for yourself and others
- ❖ Struggling because you don't have time for others

Career and creativity

- ❖ No time and space to work on your career or be creative
- ❖ Can't see what you need to do to further your career
- ❖ Believe that you have to do it all alone
- ❖ Exhausted and depleted because you don't have time for creative pursuits

Nourishing chakra 1

There are a variety of ways to get each of our chakras working properly. In addition to the Chakra Cleanse Meditation (see Chapter 28), which strengthens and balances all our chakras, each lower chakra has 'special likes' – things that 'feed' it. Engaging in these activities or indulging these likes can help to enliven these chakras.

Among the things your first chakra likes are:

- ❖ The colour red. Wear red, paint or draw with it, visualise it, add more red to your décor . . . Be creative!
- ❖ Nature
- ❖ All forms of movement (especially wild, crazy dancing)
- ❖ Anything that grounds you. You can go for long walks or hikes, spend time gardening, even hug a tree!
- ❖ Spending time in places and environments where you feel good or at home
- ❖ Spending time with people who love and support you

Remember Pauline, David and Katja? Once they began to work on their base chakras, things started to shift in their lives.

Pauline's turnaround was one of the more dramatic I've seen. It didn't happen overnight, but with regular chakra balancing and more trips to the country where she could connect with nature, Pauline saw drastic improvements in her health. She had more energy and vitality, her lower back pain and bowel issues resolved, and she began finding more satisfaction and enjoyment in her relationships.

When David began to work on his first chakra, his urge to stay 'on the move' disappeared. Realising that he felt most at home in Amsterdam, he settled there. He married a Dutch woman and they had a child, and he retired.

As for Katja, when her base chakra began to improve, so did her ability to attract more money and abundance into her life. Her ex-husband suddenly decided to buy her an apartment. Clients she hadn't spoken to for a long time began contacting her again, and her daughter phoned her out of the blue and wanted to rebuild their relationship.

Remember, chakra 1 is the keystone chakra. If it is impaired – a common issue in today's world – you cannot effectively draw energy up into the rest of your chakras. You also won't feel grounded, supported or at home.

CHAPTER 22

CHAKRA 2: INDIVIDUATION

Chakra 2 is the second level of your energy anatomy. Also called the sacral chakra, it's located in the area of your sacrum, just below your navel. While chakra 1 governs your drive to seek out that which you need to survive, chakra 2 oversees your ability to draw to yourself that which you *desire*.

Your second chakra is like a powerful magnet; when it is balanced and energised, you can easily recognise that which you desire and draw it into your life. In other words, chakra 2 magnetises your personal power so you can learn how to get what you want.

Chakra 2 is concerned with other aspects of desire as well: It oversees our sensuality, sexuality, abundance and creativity. A strong second chakra allows you to take delight in life, but helps you remain balanced in the process – you can experience joy in the sensory world without getting lost in it.

Your second chakra also helps you determine how to express yourself creatively and sexually. When chakra 2 is healthy, you regularly undertake creative activities that help you nourish your soul and express yourself as an individual. You also feel comfortable expressing yourself as a sensual and sexual being.

Considering that chakra 2 oversees sexual expression, it's not surprising that it's also the energy centre that drives you to seek out intimate relationships. These can be romantic relationships or friendships. These relationships provide the polarising forces necessary to help you learn about yourself and discover key aspects of who you are.

It may not surprise you to learn that we live in a time of massive chakra 2 imbalance. We yearn to have what we desire and what makes us feel good; our entire lives revolve around wanting and striving for more. We want to enjoy our lives and experience pleasure; we crave it. But when the second chakra is out of balance, we feel guilt and shame about wanting to feel good. And then we become trapped in cycles of addiction, yearning and striving for pleasure and what we desire. To be healthy, we need to be able to seek out and experience joy *without* feeling bad about it.

Chakra 2 basics

Names
Chakra 2 is also called the sacral chakra.

Location
It is located in the area of the sacrum, just below the level of the navel.

Areas of body governed

This chakra oversees the physical areas of the lower abdomen, pelvis, reproductive system, kidneys, bladder and the upper part of the large intestine (colon).

Drive and issues

Chakra 2 governs our drive to pursue individuation and pleasure. It is the chakra that oversees our sexuality and sensuality, and it rules the pursuit of intimate relationships. Chakra 2 drives us to engage in creative pursuits that nourish our soul, and to experience delight. It also magnetises our personal power so we can easily attract what we want.

Most people have at least some degree of imbalance in their second chakra. Let's look at some clients I've worked with who experienced chakra 2 imbalances. Then we'll explore this fiery power centre further, so you can get yours fit and healthy!

Case studies

Peter

In my work as a medical intuitive, I've always taken pride in being objective; I do my best to tell people what I see without passing judgement or imposing my own beliefs. Though I usually succeed, with some clients it's more difficult, and this is the case with Peter. When I hear his voice over the phone, I take an instant dislike to him. It's not just his voice; I also recoil at the psychic and physical impression I receive. With his large eyes, black hair and caramel-coloured skin, he probably has no trouble attracting women, but to me he seems like a creep.

Peter begins to speak, but my attention quickly strays from his words to his energy field. As I begin to scan it, the image of a huge spider rises in my mind's eye. I see that Peter creates giant webs around people to trap and then devour them. No wonder I have such a strong, negative reaction to his voice!

'I'm incredibly successful,' Peter boasts. 'Money is definitely not an issue for me.' As he talks, I see that he's a master manipulator who can get people to do whatever he wants. He uses people to fulfil his own needs. I also see that he is very sceptical about my psychic and intuitive abilities.

I stop Peter, explaining that I like to do the energy reading first, without hearing anything about his life.

'Go for it,' he says, and in my vision of him I can see his fake white teeth open into a Cheshire cat–like grin.

I focus on his energy and tell him exactly what I see, leaving nothing out.

After I'm done sharing my impressions, Peter takes a few moments before responding. 'I, uh . . .' he stammers, then clears his throat and tries again. 'Like I said, I've got lots of money,' he says, his voice now meek and shaky, 'but the truth is, it's a problem for me. I can't stop amassing wealth . . . But somehow it seems like there's never enough.'

I tell him it's his imbalanced first and second chakras – especially the second – that are causing him to feel that way. 'Your fear of scarcity is driving your need to accumulate wealth at all costs. Your second chakra is severely imbalanced.

I can see that you're just as driven to acquire pleasure, and that these drives and fears are ruining your life.'

Peter is quiet for a minute, then says, 'It's true; I spend just about all day every day working.' He tells me he's also left a trail of angry and bitter men and women who he's used to acquire power and wealth, or for sex. 'I've just gotten out of another relationship. Well, an affair, really. It never got beyond that. I'm also in the middle of another lawsuit with a former business partner.' Then he laughs. 'You know, it seems strange, but I'm actually happy that you can see all this about me. I feel relieved.'

'Because you're not honest with anyone,' I say. 'You don't have authentic relationships in your life. And on top of it, you're struggling with prostate, bladder and back problems.'

'Yes,' he says, agreeing with me once again. Peter's master manipulator mask is gone. Behind it is a frightened little boy.

'The truth is, you have a lot of money in the bank, but you're deeply afraid of life. You don't have true wealth because you have no support system – no friends or family.'

'Yes,' he says, 'that's all true.'

'You can change all this, Peter,' I tell him, 'but you've got a lot of work ahead of you.'

Nancy

Nancy comes to me via a referral from her doctor, so I am already aware that she has ongoing issues with her reproductive system, and that for decades she has been plagued with ovarian cysts, as well as chronic urinary tract infections.

'You know what my doctor told me to try for the infections?' she says. 'Drink cranberry juice. That was easy. Just add a little vodka and we're off to the races!' She throws her head back and laughs, showing off the studded leather choker around her neck.

Nancy is in her late thirties, tanned, with long, bleached-blonde hair. She's wearing a black Bon Jovi tank top, tight jeans and high leather boots with stiletto heels.

Nancy tells me she also has problems with relationships. 'All the good ones are taken! Every time I think I might have found one, he up and leaves. Oh well!' she laughs. 'Nothing a little retail therapy won't cure. Men aren't worth all the fuss, anyway.'

I don't have to scan Nancy's energy field to know what's happening — her second chakra is virtually leaping out at me, begging for help. 'You're swinging back and forth between a very undernourished and a hugely engorged second chakra,' I tell her. 'That's what's causing your childlike behaviour.'

The smile disappears from Nancy's face briefly, then returns. 'Getting old is overrated,' she fires back.

'Your issues with your second chakra are causing you to engage in some dangerous behaviour, bingeing on drugs and alcohol and engaging in unprotected sex with strangers. You're searching for a high, for acceptance, or for a way to feel alive,' I say, without judgement.

'Well, who doesn't want to feel alive?' she counters.

I don't respond. Nancy goes to say something else, then closes her mouth, her smile fading. When she speaks again, her voice is completely different, almost like a little girl's. 'What do I do?' she asks.

'Well, we need to get your second chakra in balance,' I say. 'That should help with your physical and financial problems, as well.' Nancy looks at me, clearly surprised that I can see she's got money problems. 'You're always in debt because of your shopping habit. It's another addiction — another way to get that high.'

Nancy nods but says nothing. She looks like a child who's been called to the principal's office.

'It doesn't mean you're a bad person,' I reassure her. 'You're just engaging in some unhealthy behaviour, and that's affecting your relationships too. You're trying to have relationships with grown men while acting like a teenager. There's nothing wrong with the men you're attracting into your life, you're just afraid that when they get to know you, they won't like what they see, so you start to "act up", and that drives them away.'

'Wow, you really nailed it. You must see a lot of women like me,' she says.

'Actually, I more often see women with an underactive second chakra — women who are scared of their sexuality, afraid to open themselves up and make mistakes, unwilling to be spontaneous, free, creative and impulsive . . .'

'Oh, yeah, that's definitely not me!' Nancy declares.

'No, it's not,' I say, 'but in both cases — overactive and underactive — when people get their chakras aligned and healthy, things start to make a dramatic turnaround.

And that's the only "drama" you're allowed to create now, Nancy,' I tell her. She laughs, and this time I join in.

John

Diagnosing the true source of a chakric imbalance can be a bit tricky at times, and John is a perfect example of this. In many ways, his life seems perfectly in order. He owns a popular franchise chain, and as he sits in front of me in his beautifully pressed tan trousers and jacket, he looks like the picture of success.

But John's energy field shows me something different. All his working life, John has been able to land the job he wants, and he has the resumé to prove it. He also works as a life coach and runs successful inspirational seminars. However, he's having trouble with money.

John nods when I tell him what I see. 'I don't get it,' John says, shrugging. 'I'm great at what I do, but' – he leans forward and lowers his voice, clearly embarrassed – 'there just never seems to be enough. I don't want people to know that I'm struggling,' he says. 'Who would want a coach who has trouble making money?'

'Let's take a deeper look,' I say. When I begin to scan, I see a rather significant blockage in John's second chakra. When I home in on this blockage, I see that John has an ambivalent attitude towards money, which he's inherited from his father. John's father believed that 'rich people are bad and the poor are good', so John has subconscious guilt and feels bad about his desire for money.

I tell John what I see. 'Yes,' he sighs, 'my dad always told me that an honest man works hard for his money and has just enough to get by. I know rationally that it's okay to desire money and enjoy it, but subconsciously I must still feel bad about it.'

John thinks for a few moments, crossing and uncrossing his legs, scratching his head. Finally he shrugs and says, 'Belinda, you're telling me what I already know. This is not really news to me. I've known for years this has been holding me back, and I've been trying hard to overcome it, but I can't see why it's not working. What am I doing wrong?'

'The answer to your question is twofold,' I reply. 'First, your ambivalent feeling about money is certainly one of the reasons you're struggling financially, but it isn't the only one. And second, although you've been trying to change your thoughts, that hasn't yet changed your energy. I'll teach you how to clear out these blockages and change your energy.'

'So what's my real problem, then?' he says, leaning forward.

'Unrequited love,' I say. John's mouth opens slightly in surprise. 'In a past life,' I continue, 'you were in love with a woman who didn't desire you. Although you tried for many years to win her affections, she chose another man, married him and they moved away. Yet you still believed that the two of you were destined to be together, so you began to pray vigilantly every night for God to bring her back to you. Thus began a recurring dream; a dream in which your beloved showed up at your house one day, asking for forgiveness and asking you to accept her as your bride.'

169

John sits spellbound as I continue. I tell him that, convinced his visions predicted the future, he anxiously awaited her return. And it happened soon enough.

John opened the door of his house one day to find her on his doorstep, pale-faced and crying. Her husband and child had been badly injured in an accident with their cart and wagon nearby. She begged John to come and help them.

John was convinced that his beloved was making up this tale so she could get him away from the prying eyes and wagging tongues of his neighbours; he was sure she would lead him down into the village where she could profess her love and dedication to him privately. Eagerly, he followed her out of the village gate and onto the road.

When he stepped out of the village gate he saw that, indeed, a wagon lay overturned on the street and a man and small boy lay on the ground, unconscious. John was confused. Suddenly, he realised that his beloved was telling the truth, and that she was not his beloved after all!

John fell to his knees wailing, feeling tricked and betrayed by love and hope and God. He then suffered a severe stroke and spent the rest of that life alone and isolated.

When I finish, John is holding back tears. 'I can't believe what you're telling me,' he whispers. 'This is exactly what's happening in my life right now! My girlfriend has left me for another man. Although she's told me it's over and that she wants to be with him and not me, I can't give up on her because I love her and believe we're destined to be together. I dream every night that she comes back to me, professing her love and apologising for her mistake.'

'But that's not all,' he continues. 'This has also happened to me in my previous relationships. My girlfriends have all ended the relationship, and each time I hoped and believed they would come back because we were destined to be together. But they never did come back, no matter how much I believed they would, and I've felt betrayed by my own hope and faith. Now I realise that all this time, I've been living out a wound from a past life!'

He sits there, arms crossed, processing what he's just learned. 'So,' he says, after a long pause, 'I understand how this past-life wound has affected my relationships, but what does this have to do with my money problems?'

'The job of your second chakra is to make sure you can attract into your life that which you desire,' I say, 'and money is a part of that. Because you deeply desired this woman and thought that God/the universe would give her to you, and God/the universe didn't, you've internalised a message that says your deepest desires will not be fulfilled. Your father's negative beliefs about money only served to cement this belief in your energy field.'

John is awestruck. 'Who would have thought that unrequited love in a past life could stop the flow of money into my life in this one? I never would have made that connection, but now that you say it, it makes perfect sense!'

It's obvious that John needs to clear out the pain of this past life, as well as work on his chakras. I teach him how to do this, advising him to pay particular attention to his second chakra. He promises to stick with the practices.

As you can see, chakric imbalances can present in many ways. John's example in particular illustrates that what at first may seem to be the problem (in his case, money) could actually be the result of another issue entirely.

Don't worry – you don't have to be psychic to figure these things out (though over time, your work with the Chakra Cleanse Meditation can help to enhance your intuitive abilities). Once you develop a thorough understanding of the various aspects of each chakra and start working with them regularly, getting to the bottom of these issues gets easier.

Now let's look at chakra 2 in detail.

Chakra 2 self-assessment

To get an idea of how fit and healthy your second chakra is, ask yourself the following questions:

Y / N Can I easily manifest that which I desire in life?

Y / N Do I have a sense of my individual identity and what I want?

Y / N Am I willing to explore life and find out more about myself?

Y / N Do I enjoy my life, and can I take pleasure in the small things?

Y / N Can I express myself sexually? Am I sexually fulfilled?

Y / N Can I express myself creatively? Am I creatively fulfilled?

Y / N Do I honour my creativity by making time for play?

Y / N Can I let go and simply enjoy life?

Y / N Am I free from problems with my reproductive system, kidneys, bladder and colon?

If you answered 'no' to a few of these questions, you have some challenges with your second chakra. If you answered 'no' to many of them, you probably have a significant blockage.

Chakra 2 out of balance

If your second chakra is not working properly, you may have challenges with your physical or emotional health, finances, love life, relationships with family and friends or your career and creativity. It's important to note that an imbalance in one chakra will likely affect the energy flow to the chakras above and below it. So if you have a weak or blocked chakra 2, you may experience one or more of the chakra 1 problems as well.

The following are some challenges you may experience if your second chakra is imbalanced.

Physical health

❖ Gynaecological issues, such as ovarian cysts or endometriosis
❖ Some fertility and sexual issues, sexually transmitted diseases, low libido, menstrual problems, pain or PMS
❖ Bladder, kidney or pelvis issues
❖ Chronic lower back pain, including sciatica

Emotional health

❖ Excessive feelings of shame or guilt
❖ Feeling alienated or cut off from others
❖ Mood swings
❖ Addictive behaviours
❖ Unhealthy promiscuity or frigidity
❖ Envy

❖ Denial and judgement
❖ Issues with boundaries, such as having no or ill-defined boundaries, or intruding on others' boundaries

Finances
❖ Feel bad about wanting money
❖ Obsessively attached to money
❖ Don't have enough money to enjoy life's pleasures
❖ Frugality
❖ Spending binges

Love life
❖ Intimacy and sexual issues, such as frigidity, promiscuity or being sexually demanding
❖ Untrusting, feeling like the other person is after something
❖ Inability to feel safe and secure and trust yourself, others and life
❖ Looking for a partner to make you feel better
❖ Choosing partners for selfish or immature reasons, such as someone who makes you look good
❖ Libido that is too low or too high

Relationships with friends and family
❖ Can't be open or honest
❖ Can't give physical affection
❖ Withdrawn, shy or untrusting
❖ Selfish or demanding
❖ Irresponsible or emotionally unstable
❖ Manipulative

Career and creativity

❖ Lack of creativity
❖ Can't feel and express joy
❖ Lack of ability to stop and smell the roses
❖ Excessive creativity, to the extent that you are not functioning in the real world and meeting your daily needs
❖ Self-absorbed
❖ Climbing the career ladder to get ahead and 'be someone or something', or great aspirations to be a celebrity or otherwise well-known

Nourishing chakra 2

In addition to doing the Chakra Cleanse Meditation (see Chapter 28), engaging in these activities or indulging these 'likes' can help enliven your second chakra:

❖ The colour orange
❖ Beautiful environments, such as art galleries, botanical gardens and old Gothic churches
❖ Massage, hugs and lovemaking
❖ Romance
❖ Gorgeous, breathtaking sunsets
❖ Losing yourself in the fullness and beauty of the present moment
❖ Dancing naked
❖ Anything that you find delightful

Remember Peter, Nancy and John? With some diligent work, including an extra focus on their second chakras, beautiful changes started happening in their lives.

I told Peter that he had a lot of work to do on himself, and I'm happy to report he did it. The next time I spoke with him, he told me he was changing his life by changing his chakras. I knew he was telling me the truth because when I heard his voice, I no longer had the instinct to get far away from him!

Nancy too had a long road ahead of her. After a few stops and starts, she was finally able to make a routine of working with her chakras. When I spoke with her a year after her session, she had been alcohol- and drug-free for three months, and was working on repairing several of her friendships. She was dating a new man, and though it was challenging at times, she was sticking to her new mantra: 'No drama!'

When I last spoke with John, he was experiencing much more financial stability, and he was happily single. He'd decided to stop pining for love and would no longer allow himself to think about the past or miss his ex-girlfriends. He had started anew and was enjoying his time as a bachelor.

CHAPTER 23

CHAKRA 3: STRENGTH

Chakra 3 is the third level of your energy anatomy. Also called the solar plexus chakra, it is located in the area of your stomach. Where chakra 1 governs your drive to meet your survival needs and chakra 2 oversees your ability to manifest that which you desire, chakra 3 governs your ability to make your way in the world and to stand up for what you want. It helps you know what is right for you, and to live it.

Your third chakra is the energy centre that generates self-esteem and self-empowerment. When you have a healthy sense of self-esteem, you recognise what empowers you, and make choices that are in your best interests. Your third chakra enables you to set healthy boundaries and to protect yourself by saying 'no' to unhealthy people and situations.

You can think of chakra 3 as your bodyguard. It helps you detect unhealthy people and situations, and sense when a person's energy is negative or encroaching on yours. The gut feeling that someone or something isn't good for you or that someone is draining your energy is your third chakra talking.

In addition to alerting us to negative and potentially dangerous situations and people, chakra 3 is also where you create your personal honour code and generate the willpower to stick by it. If you lack self-esteem, you tend to let others dictate what happens to you. A powerful third chakra enables you to stand up for what you want and what you believe in, while still being able to compromise from a place of self-empowerment.

Chakra 3 basics

Names
Chakra 3 is also called the solar plexus chakra.

Location
It is located in the area of the stomach.

Areas of body governed
This chakra oversees the physical areas of the stomach, liver, gallbladder, digestive system and spleen.

Drive and issues
Chakra 3 generates your personal power and helps you maintain strong, healthy boundaries. This chakra also oversees your self-esteem and sense of self-empowerment. Chakra 3 is where you set your moral code and generate the resolve to stick to it by standing up for yourself and what you believe in.

Like chakra 2, chakra 3 is another area where weaknesses are common; many people struggle with their third chakra. (Think of how many people you know who have solid, healthy boundaries versus those who don't.) To get an idea of how a chakra 3 imbalance can affect your life, let's look at a few of my past clients.

Case studies

Laura

Laura is a quiet woman with a shy demeanour. She looks as if she'd like nothing more than to disappear into the pattern of the chair. She's slouched forward, arms crossed, and everything about her seems drab and downcast, even the beige tones of her sweater and leggings.

When I look at Laura's energy field, I can see she is suffering badly from a recent break-up. She routinely gives all of herself in relationships, but always ends up broken-hearted. As well as being sad, she's also confused about why this keeps happening.

With Laura in so much pain, I take extra care in how I talk to her about it. Instead of telling her everything I know, I start slowly. 'Laura, I see you're in a difficult spot because of a recent break-up.'

'Yes,' she says and winces, then takes a deep breath. 'I don't know what's wrong with me. I'm such a loving person. I take good care of my partners, but it never seems to work out. All I want to do is find someone who can receive what I have to give.'

Laura works as an acupuncturist, running a busy community clinic where people can receive treatments on a discounted basis. She gives her all to her clients as well, often working overtime.

'When's the last time you said "no" to someone, Laura?' I ask her.

'What?' she says and straightens a little, clearly caught off guard. 'What do you mean?'

'I mean you're severely lacking boundaries,' I say. 'I can hear it in your words, but your energy field also shows me that you have almost no willpower. And your self-esteem is weak. Laura, do you know who you are?'

'I don't know what you . . .' she starts to say, but trails off. She reaches up and rubs her necklace. It's a gesture I've seen her make several times since arriving. 'I guess you're right,' she finally says.

'Your third chakra is extremely weak,' I continue. 'You need to learn to create boundaries in your relationships and stop letting people – especially men – walk all over you. You've got to learn to stand up for yourself and say what you want.'

'But I gave him everything he wanted,' she sobs. 'I gave everything, and even that wasn't enough!'

'Maybe that was the problem,' I say. 'Perhaps he stopped respecting you.' She looks at me, but says nothing. 'You've got "empath syndrome",' I continue. 'You have a big heart and are sensitive to others' feelings, so you want to help everyone. But you haven't got the boundaries or discernment necessary to make wise choices about who to help *and how. And worst of all – you're not caring for yourself. That's why you're tired all the time. You've got adrenal fatigue from working so hard, and you're letting others take all your energy. We have got to get you grounded and in a space where you can be more discerning with your heart and your healing talents.'*

'But . . .' she starts to say, then trails off again. Finally, she nods. 'Okay,' she says. 'Show me how.'

'You're going to start by turning that love you have inward and focusing on yourself,' I tell her. 'We're going to get your third chakra nice and fit so you have greater self-esteem, along with better judgement about where to spend your precious heart energy.'

Barbara

The first thing that strikes me about Barbara is her grouchy mood. I'm speaking to her on the phone, and as she says 'Hello', I instantly receive the visual impression of a woman who is overweight, tired and grumpy. Normally, I have a more formal way of starting my sessions, but I can sense that Barbara is someone who likes people to give it to her straight. I say, 'Barbara, you're tired of being cranky and overweight. You want to know how to change.'

Through the earpiece I hear an outburst of sharp laughter. 'Too right!' she declares.

'You also feel like people take advantage of you, but you have a hard time telling them this. So instead you just find ways to shut them out and use food to comfort yourself.'

'I know I don't eat well,' Barbara counters. 'Plenty of doctors have told me that. What else can you tell me?'

'You're stuffing yourself with these foods because your fourth chakra is being starved of love. You need to feel that loving energy in your heart chakra.

'You need healthy relationships in your life. You need love and companionship. We all do. I can see that your true nature is warm and caring, but your experiences have made you hard and mean. You take your frustration out on others, and I can see that you don't like this about yourself.'

'Okay,' Barbara says, 'you're right again, about all of it. What else?'

'I can see as I scan your energy field that in addition to not having healthy relationships, you're having some problems with your physical health that are contributing to you being overweight,' I continue. 'Your third, fourth and fifth chakras are weak and blocked, particularly your third chakra. In fact, they're so blocked that it would be almost impossible for you not to feel angry and frustrated. But beyond that, I can see in your third chakra that your liver is exhausted; it's desperately trying to do its job, and so is your pancreas, but both these organs are struggling with all the sugary and fatty foods you're consuming. It's too much for them to process.'

'Wow,' she says.

'Plus I'm seeing in your fifth chakra – in the area of your throat – that your thyroid and hormonal levels are very imbalanced. You really need to go to an endocrinologist to help you get that sorted.'

'Great,' she grumbles, 'another doctor.'

'Look, Barbara, I know you've had some bad experiences with doctors, but this really will help. We've got to get those hormones balanced, plus get these blockages cleared from your chakras so the energy can flow and you can release this anger.'

'Fine,' she sighs.

'Barbara, I mean it,' I say.

'Okay, okay,' she laughs. 'What do I do?'

I explain the chakra system to Barbara and outline how to start cleansing her chakras. I tell her it's going to take some faith on her part to keep with it because she's got a lot of healing to do. As we end the session, Barbara also promises to see an endocrinologist straight away.

Simone

'I can't stand my boss,' Simone says the moment she sits down. 'She's ruining my life and I hate my work.' She sits rigid and upright, clutching her purse in her lap. Everything about her looks tight. Her lips are pursed, her knees and ankles are clamped together, and her blouse is buttoned all the way to the top of her neck.

'Okay,' I say. 'I can tell you're anxious to get going, but let me start by telling you what I tell all my clients – it's better for you not to give me any information. I like to get a clean impression from your energy field without being influenced by anything you might say. How about you get comfortable, and I'll look at your energy field and see what's happening.'

'She's terrible,' Simone continues, her features pinched so tight her eyes are squinting. 'It's like she —'

I hold up a hand. 'Let me just take a look first and see what your energy field is showing me. Then we can talk about your boss.'

When I look at Simone's energy field, I certainly see what she's talking about — she really can't stand her boss. She thinks almost nonstop about how mean her boss is, how unfairly she treats Simone, how demanding she is and how she fails to recognise all that Simone does.

Simone's third chakra is heavily depleted, not only because she focuses incessantly on how much she dislikes her boss, but also because she feels powerless to change her work situation.

'You think too much about your boss,' I tell her. 'This is making you tired and sick. It's giving you an upset stomach, and it's making you irritable, which you often take out on your children.'

'Of course I think too much about my boss,' she says, sitting upright again. 'You would too, if you had to work with her!'

'Here's the thing,' I explain. 'I can also see that your boss is the type of person who respects people who stand up for themselves. You need to show her that you're strong. The problem is that you're so stressed about your boss, you feel weak and depleted, and that's encouraging her to be even more dominant. You've got to show her some backbone.'

Simone thinks for a minute. When she speaks again, her voice has lost some of its edge. 'She's just so pushy and forceful.'

'I know,' I say, 'but you've got to learn to hold your own.'

Simone offers a little more resistance. 'But she deserves to be thought badly of!' she says. I point out that this attitude is only serving to deplete Simone and lessen her power in her boss's eyes.

'Spending all this time thinking bad thoughts about someone else wastes your own precious energy. It's wearing you out!' I say.

Finally, something clicks. 'Yes,' she nods. 'That does make sense. I think I'm starting to understand what you're talking about. It's tiring. Exhausting, in fact.'

I take Simone through an exercise on holding her centre – called 'shielding' – which is designed to energise the third chakra. 'This, along with the chakra cleansing and strengthening I described, will help you hold a firm line with her.'

'Let's hope,' Simone says. For the first time, she seems to relax a bit, even offering a hint of a smile.

'Keep me posted,' I say. 'I definitely want to hear how this works out.'

Chakra 3 self-assessment

To get an idea of how fit and healthy your third chakra is, ask yourself the following questions:

Y / N Can I say 'no' and stand up for what I believe in?

Y / N Do I have healthy self-esteem? Am I self-confident?

Y / N Can I 'hold my centre', feeling balanced and sure of myself in spite of other people's thoughts and emotions?

Y / N Can I put my mind to something and follow it through?

Y / N Do I have a sense of what is good for me?

Y / N Do I have a moral code, and do I live by it?

Y / N Can I set boundaries emotionally?

Y / N Can I protect myself from taking on other people's lower energies?

Y / N Can I protect myself from feeling overly responsible for other people's lives/emotions?

Y / N Am I motivated, and do I feel empowered?

Y / N Can I hold my ground instead of giving away power to avoid confrontation?

Y / N Am I free of digestive problems and anxiety attacks?

If you answered 'no' to a few of these questions, you have some challenges with your third chakra. If you answered 'no' to many of them, you probably have a significant blockage.

Chakra 3 out of balance

If your third chakra is not working properly, you may have challenges with your physical or emotional health, finances, love life, relationships with family and friends or your career and creativity. Remember, an imbalance in one chakra will likely affect the energy flow to the chakras above and below it. So if you have a weak or blocked chakra 3, you may experience one or more of the problems related to chakras 1 and 2 as well.

The following are some challenges you could experience if your third chakra is imbalanced.

Physical health

- ❖ Stomach ulcer
- ❖ Liver problems
- ❖ Diabetes, pancreatitis or hypoglycemia
- ❖ Irritable bowel syndrome, frequent vomiting or a 'nervous stomach'
- ❖ Colon and intestinal problems
- ❖ Adrenal/chronic fatigue

Emotional health

- ❖ Low self-esteem
- ❖ Inability to care for yourself
- ❖ Feeling overly responsible for others, enmeshed in others' lives and energy
- ❖ Fearful or experiencing panic attacks
- ❖ Feeling weak or trapped
- ❖ Disempowered
- ❖ Taking the victim role, passive and blaming
- ❖ Overly aggressive
- ❖ Controlling or stubborn
- ❖ Exhibit bullying behaviours
- ❖ Over functioning and competitive

Finances

- ❖ Don't feel worthy to charge adequate prices or ask for a raise
- ❖ Lack self-discipline and follow-through
- ❖ Don't know what career or path is right for you
- ❖ Don't receive the abundance of the universe

Love life

- ❖ Don't feel worthy, and spend time with toxic people
- ❖ Victim of 'energy vampirism'
- ❖ Frequent communication difficulties
- ❖ Passive aggressive
- ❖ Fight/conflict, engage in battle of wills
- ❖ Controlled or are controlling
- ❖ Lack of equality in relationships
- ❖ Too trusting, open or loving with unsafe people
- ❖ Emotionally confused/confuse others
- ❖ Blaming or aggressive

Relationships with friends and family

- ❖ Frequent communication issues
- ❖ Controlled or are controlling
- ❖ Fight/conflict, engage in battle of wills
- ❖ Estranged from family
- ❖ Frightened of conflict or saying what you want
- ❖ Reluctance to be honest with people
- ❖ Lack of transparency or openness

Career and creativity

- ❖ Lack clarity and direction; difficulty knowing what is right for you
- ❖ Self-absorbed, won't work as part of a team
- ❖ Lack self-discipline or motivation
- ❖ Lack self-esteem and confidence to share your creative ideas with others

Nourishing chakra 3

Participating in the following activities or indulging these 'likes' can help to enliven your third chakra:

❖ The colour yellow
❖ Saying 'no' if something isn't right for you
❖ Martial arts
❖ 'Holding your centre' when confronted with a differing opinion and responding only when you know your own truth
❖ Focus, persistence and diligence
❖ Diplomacy and strength of character
❖ Acting like a 'peaceful warrior' – someone who stands in a quiet place of power and strength

So what happened with Laura, Barbara and Simone? I'm happy to say that the last time I spoke with them, all three were doing much better.

Laura had cut back on her hours at the clinic and had taken on another acupuncturist as a business partner. With someone to share the workload, she felt much better about working fewer hours and taking time off for a much-needed vacation. She had also become more discriminating about who she dated, having realised that for years she'd chosen men based on the subconscious perception that they needed her help. Now, she sought a balanced relationship instead of one based on saving her partner.

Barbara did go to get her hormones tested straight away, and the test confirmed that her hormonal levels were very imbalanced. In fact, I later spoke with the doctor myself, and he told me that Barbara's were the most imbalanced levels she'd ever seen! Barbara began a liver and pancreas detox program and kept up with the chakra cleansing and strengthening. In six months her health had greatly improved, and so had her mood.

As for Simone, in a short space of time – and to her amazement – her boss began acting differently around her. She now rarely yelled at Simone or criticised her, and when her boss was in one of her moods, Simone simply let her be and got on with her own day, not allowing herself to waste her precious time being angry or upset. Simone's stomach pains went away, she could sleep better and she had worked out how to better balance her home and work life.

CHAPTER 24

CHAKRA 4: LOVE

Chakra 4 is the fourth level of your energy anatomy. Also called the heart chakra (because of its location), it is one of the most, if not *the* most important of your chakras. It governs all your emotions, especially love.

Chakras 3 and 4 work together closely in several ways. In chakra 3, you learn what it means to have self-esteem and self-confidence, as well as discernment. How to be a peaceful warrior — someone who stands quietly but powerfully in a place of strength. It is in chakra 4 that you learn to *deepen* your ability to be a peaceful warrior, as this chakra generates compassion and empathy, and governs how you become a vehicle and vessel for love. The heart chakra is the source of unconditional love without judgement, while the solar plexus chakra applies discernment to where and how you channel that love.

Your fourth chakra is selfless in terms of loving others, but it's also focused on unconditional self-love. To truly love and accept others and be free of ego, you must truly love and accept yourself. Achieving this, you become a vehicle for great healing and transformation; when you let go of the sense of separateness created by the ego, you are free to connect to everyone and everything.

A balanced heart chakra also cleans your energy field of emotional negativity, so it's vital that this chakra works. Otherwise you become emotionally and psychically polluted.

Chakra 4 basics

Names
Chakra 4 is also called the heart chakra.

Location
It is located in the area of the heart.

Areas of body governed
This chakra oversees the physical areas of the heart, blood, chest, hands and arms, lungs and circulatory system.

Drive and issues
Chakra 4 oversees all our emotions, especially the pursuit and expression of love. It is concerned with giving and receiving love to others and to yourself, as well as compassion, forgiveness and acceptance.

An imbalanced or weak heart chakra can affect your life in many ways. To see examples of these effects, let's look at some of my clients who have had challenges with chakra 4.

Case studies
Anna

My first impression of Anna is so clear and sad, it makes my heart ache. I'm speaking to her on the phone, and as I tell her what she can expect from our session, I'm distracted by an image that's coming to me so strongly it's difficult to concentrate on what I'm saying.

I see Anna, who looks to be in her thirties, wearing a simple, faded dress with her straight brown hair tied back in a loose ponytail at the nape of her neck. She sits at a window, looking out on the world. Outside is a beautiful garden filled with flowers, and there are animals playing and children laughing. Suddenly Anna calls out to the children, 'Here I am! Can I come play with you?' She yells through the glass, but the children can't hear her.

I watch as Anna searches the room, looking for a way out, but she can't find one. Finally, she gives up. She slumps to the floor, covers her face with her hands and begins to weep.

I take a deep breath, trying to maintain my composure, but the vision of Anna is so sad it's difficult to hold back the tears. 'Anna,' I say, 'I can see in your energy field that you had dreams for your life that haven't come true. As a result, you've shut down your heart to try to protect yourself from getting hurt again.'

Anna begins to cry. 'I don't have anyone in my life,' she says. 'I'm all alone, but I'm afraid to reach out to anyone.'

'You're suffering from a broken heart chakra,' I continue, 'and because you've shut down your heart, you've blocked the flow of love into your life. In fact, you've shut it down so thoroughly that you've blocked the flow of everything good into your life. That's why you're struggling with money.'

'I don't know what to do,' she sobs. 'I don't even know how to connect with people anymore; the thought of it terrifies me.'

I know Anna has been trying to heal, but her repeated failures have only made her shut down further. She was referred to me by her psychologist, who feared she was no longer making progress with Anna.

'Well, Anna, I have some good news for you. I'm not going to tell you to go out and talk to people.'

The telephone line is quiet for a moment. 'You're not?' she finally says, sounding slightly suspicious.

'Instead, we're going to work on healing your heart chakra. Then it won't be such a struggle to try and interact with people.'

'But . . . I'm scared,' she says.

'I understand,' I reply, 'because your third chakra is also very weak. Chakra 3 is critical to being able to love openly because it's the chakra that protects your heart. If your third chakra isn't working, your heart can't open safely. In fact, your first and second chakras could also use some support, but don't worry — we'll address all of them.

Once energy flows freely through your chakras, you'll feel safe, more grounded, more confident and more willing to let people in again. Once we get the love moving into your life again, Anna, all sorts of good things will start to flow to you. How does that sound?'

'Still scary,' Anna says, 'but also really good.'

Luke

When Luke walks into the room, suddenly things feel stuffy. For a moment, I wonder if I'm coming down with something; out of nowhere I feel too warm and as if I'm having trouble breathing. A few moments later, I understand why.

As Luke settles into the chair, I start to receive images and information from his energy field. He certainly seems likeable enough, and he's young, handsome and well groomed. But I can see in his energy that he's having trouble with his relationships, and that the women in his past have found him needy and suffocating. No wonder I feel this way!

I take a sip of water to help shake the feeling, then explain to Luke how the session will go. 'I can't wait!' he smiles. 'I'll be so happy if you can help me.'

'For starters,' I say, 'you feel you're having trouble meeting the right woman. You've already had lots of relationships, but none of them have gone the way you'd hoped, so you've recently given up.'

'That's right,' he says, shaking his head wistfully. 'Relationships just don't seem to work for me.'

'Your past hurts have caused a blockage in your heart chakra – you're afraid to love again because you're afraid to get hurt, and that's creating a self-fulfilling prophecy. I can see that you're very resilient – you've "toughened up" to deal with these hurts. But that toughness has also numbed you and has made it difficult for that love energy to move easily through your life.'

'Yes, that makes sense. But . . . I don't know, I don't want to be rude . . . That doesn't sound that complicated. I mean, I think I could have figured it out on my own.' Luke looks slightly tense as he anticipates my reaction.

I smile. 'Well, yes, perhaps you could have . . . But there's more I want to tell you.'

'Yes?!' he says, leaning forward. I can't help but smile at his wide-eyed anticipation.

'Your second chakra is showing me a blockage there as well. It's to do with your mother.' His smile fades and he looks slightly deflated, but he says nothing. I can see that Luke's mother passed away when he was only eleven years old. The event was so traumatic that it stunted his emotional development. He still harbours feelings of abandonment, especially because she died just as he was moving into puberty – a time of enormous change. He couldn't experience the normal developmental milestone of transitioning from emotional dependence on his mother to independence. I tell him all this, then add, 'Because of this unresolved transition, you've been looking for your mother in your romantic relationships.'

I give him a moment to take that in, then ask him some questions about his previous relationships to help *him see this pattern: Were they mature women, older than you? Were they compassionate women who looked after you? Did you want to move in with them or have them move in with you very soon into the relationship? Were you emotionally dependent upon them? Did you expect them to solve your problems for you and protect you?*

'I'm seeing it now,' Luke says. 'So many things are starting to make sense all of a sudden. I really have been looking for my mother all this time, and that's what's made my relationships fail.' Then he gives a sharp laugh. 'When my last girlfriend broke up with me, she even said, "I'm not your mother!" I accused her of being dramatic, but she was right.'

'And how has your sex life been?' I ask, catching him off guard.

'Great . . . at first. Then after a couple of weeks, things always seem to fizzle out. It felt like my girlfriends weren't attracted to me anymore.'

'Well, I can tell you that no woman finds it sexy going to bed with someone who thinks they're their mother!'

He smiles and nods, then asks, 'But what can I do about this? How do I resolve these mother issues I have?'

'It might seem counterintuitive,' I say, 'but we're not going to worry about your mother issues – that is, we're not going to focus on your past experiences. Instead, we're going to focus on healing your chakras so they draw energy into your life to support healthier relationships and help you feel that independence you've been seeking. Once that happens, you'll find yourself relating differently to women.'

'Thank goodness!' Luke says. He leans back in the chair, obviously relieved.

Jane

Jane is exhausted; I can see it in every aspect of her energy field. By outward appearances, though, she's got everything together. She's a middle-aged woman, well dressed, with her hair and make-up done beautifully. She sits down, smiling, with her legs crossed and hands folded, and I'm struck by the sharp contrast between her physical presentation and what I see in her chakras.

I give Jane my usual introductory speech, then begin to scan her energy field more deeply. Right away I see that her first and second chakras are pale and severely depleted, and across her fourth chakra is a giant auric tear.

'You work as a caregiver,' I say.

'Yes, at the nursing home,' she says.

'You're very good at it, but you're giving too much of yourself. That's why you're exhausted. Your lower chakras are completely drained, and there's nothing left for you.'

Jane's smile begins to fade as her eyes tear up. 'It's true; I am exhausted.' She takes a moment to collect herself before continuing. 'I just care about my patients so much. Sometimes I stay past my shift. I can't help it — I'm the only "family" some of them have.' She pulls out a tissue and dabs at her eyes.

'I understand,' I say, 'but you're so depleted you're starting to get sick. Jane, you have "healer syndrome".

You are a powerful healer, yet you're helping people by giving them your own energy. That is a big no-no.' I smile, and Jane smiles back in a way that says she knows what I'm talking about. 'Healers need to channel the abundant energy of the universe,' I continue, 'not give to others from their personal supply. That energy is meant for you, to keep you going and healthy. Does that make sense?'

'Yes,' she replies, again dabbing her tired eyes with the tissue.

'Healers have big hearts and want to help people, but you have to be wise about how you're doing it, and how much you're doing it.'

'But how can I say "no" to someone who needs me?' she asks, and I can see in her energy field just what a truly caring person she is.

'There is no shame in saying "no", and protecting yourself, Jane. I know it's hard, but you've got to show some discernment about how much of yourself you give. You need boundaries.'

Jane nods. 'And I think you need a break from your work,' I add. 'A long one.'

'I feel guilty saying this, but sometimes I think about retiring.'

'Yes,' I say, 'I would seriously consider it. Energetically, you can't take it anymore. I know you love your job and you've helped a lot of people, but you've given enough. Once you recover, there are other ways you can help people — ways that are safer for you. In the meantime, I'm going to show you how to get your energy back and build up those boundaries!'

Chakra 4 self-assessment

To get an idea of how fit and healthy your fourth chakra is, ask yourself the following questions:

Y / N Do I practise self-love?

Y / N Do I feel connected to others?

Y / N Am I free from past hurts? Have I let go of feelings of betrayal, disappointment or bitterness?

Y / N Can I forgive and accept myself and others?

Y / N Can I be generous and joyous?

Y / N Can I enjoy other people for who they are, or do I always find fault in others?

Y / N Do I have heartfelt, intimate, thriving, supportive relationships in my life?

Y / N Have I found what I love and am passionate about?

Y / N Can I give and receive physical affection, such as hugs?

Y / N Can I love unconditionally, without strings attached?

Y / N Does the Law of Resonance work for me? Can I draw into my life what (and who) I love?

Y / N Do I have a healthy heart, chest, lungs and circulatory system?

If you answered 'no' to a few of these questions, you have some challenges with your fourth chakra. If you answered 'no' to many of them, you probably have a significant blockage.

Chakra 4 out of balance

If your fourth chakra is not working properly, you may have challenges with your physical or emotional health, finances, love life, relationships with family and friends or your career and creativity. Remember, an imbalance in one chakra will likely affect the energy flow to the chakras above and below it. For example, if you have a weak or blocked chakra 4, you may experience one or more of the problems related to chakras 1 to 3 as well.

The following are some challenges you will experience if your fourth chakra is imbalanced.

Physical health
❖ Heart issues, such as high blood pressure, heart murmur, heart disease or circulation problems
❖ Chest problems, such as pneumonia
❖ Breast issues
❖ Allergies
❖ Chest, shoulder, diaphragm, upper back or arm pain

Emotional health
❖ Emotionally closed down
❖ Isolated/withdrawn and lonely, brooding
❖ Highly judgemental or critical
❖ Depressed, lack of joy and lightness
❖ Fear/lack of intimate relationships, unable to trust
❖ Secretly yearn to be loved and get affection
❖ Unwillingness to forgive and move on
❖ Grief, bitterness, regret or rage
❖ Focused on trying to find love externally
❖ Clingy, needy
❖ Demanding, attached

❖ Co-dependent, martyr
❖ Sense of self/identity is role-related: 'the wife', 'the mother', 'the husband'
❖ Obsession with being a 'good and giving' person

Finances

❖ Aren't making money doing what you love
❖ Lack of generosity, compassion and genuine love and concern
❖ Can't maximise the Law of Resonance
❖ Inability to give and receive money joyfully

Love life

❖ Can't have flourishing relationships
❖ Unrealistic expectations, high standards, pressure for your partner to be perfect
❖ Often feel hurt, disappointed or betrayed
❖ Can't accept another person fully, or forgive
❖ Hypercritical, building resentments and bitterness
❖ Have toxic relationships
❖ Look externally to find the love you don't have for yourself
❖ Need other people to behave in certain ways to make you feel loved

Relationships with friends and family

❖ Similar issues as with romantic relationships
❖ Unrealistic expectations, high standards, pressure for your family to be perfect
❖ Often feel hurt, disappointed or betrayed
❖ Can't let another person be who they are

Career and creativity

❖ Lack of connection with your work
❖ Lack of joy in your work
❖ Don't do what you love

Nourishing chakra 4

Among the activities and indulgences your fourth chakra enjoys are:

❖ The colour green
❖ Heartfelt hugs, talks and movies
❖ Practising forgiveness
❖ Practising gratitude
❖ Letting go of old hurts
❖ Smiles, kind words and compassion
❖ A daily visualisation of everyone on the planet living in health, harmony and plenty
❖ Telling your loved ones how much you love them
❖ Random acts of kindness and prayer
❖ Undertaking any activities that you love

Anna, Luke and Jane all experienced significant improvements after learning how to work with their chakras and making some much-needed changes in their lives.

Together with her psychologist, I helped Anna begin to open up her heart. I showed her how to cleanse and strengthen her chakras, paying particular attention to her heart chakra, and her psychologist led her through a process where she released her old wounds and forgave others. The last time

I spoke with Anna, she proudly told me that she had joined a choir and was working at a local charity. She was also planning to study psychology and had moved back to the country of her birth.

Luke was so excited to get working on his chakras that I knew he'd have a quick turnaround, and he did. When I spoke to him several months later, he felt more confident about himself in general, and had just started to date again after taking some time off to work on himself.

When I spoke to Jane, I found that she had in fact retired. She felt more energised and was enjoying spending time rediscovering the things she loved, like gardening and decorating her house. She'd even joined a card club, gathering with neighbours every week to play bridge.

CHAPTER 25

CHAKRA 5: EXPRESSION

Chakra 5 is the fifth level of your energy anatomy. Also called the throat chakra, it oversees your communication, and it's from here that you express yourself authentically, individually and creatively.

Your fifth chakra is about honest communication and being able to communicate your needs and desires. When your fifth chakra is strong and balanced, you can express yourself truthfully and lovingly. A balanced chakra 5 also allows expression of spirituality and creativity, and helps you remain open-minded, keeping you from holding so strongly to your beliefs that you're closed to change.

This chakra also governs your will. In chakra 3, you develop your sense of willpower, such as sticking to a diet or standing up for your beliefs. Chakra 5, however, is about surrendering your personal will to divine will. When you are guided by your soul's will, you invite a higher consciousness to enter your psyche, which empowers you to speak 'your truth' and enact meaningful change in the world.

Chakra 5 basics

Names

Chakra 5 is also called the throat chakra.

Location

It is located in the area of the throat.

Areas of body governed

This chakra oversees the physical areas of the throat, neck, jaw, teeth, thyroid glands and vocal cords.

Drive and issues

Chakra 5 governs your drive to express yourself authentically and originally. It oversees your self-determination, will and ability to speak your truth.

Throat chakra issues can affect your life in many ways. To see examples of these effects, let's look at some clients I've worked with who have had challenges with their fifth chakra.

Case studies

Paul

'You're feeling depressed because you hate your job,' I tell Paul. 'And I'm not surprised, because I can see that you're

clearly in the wrong field. What is it that you do for a living?'

'IT,' he replies flatly. We're speaking on the phone, but while I can't 'see' Paul, I have a strong visual impression of him and it does not show him sitting in front of a computer. Rather, it is of him performing. His career is a mismatch for him!

'I'm sorry,' I say, 'It's just that I can see you in front of people as an entertainer. I can also clearly see that you're a painter, and quite a gifted one. IT is just so wrong for you, like a polar bear sitting on the beach trying to get a tan!'

Paul begins to laugh, seeing the absurdity of the situation. 'You've got massive blockages in your third and fifth chakras, Paul. They've gone on strike.'

'On strike?' he laughs. Paul's a good sport. I realise I'm putting a lot out there, but his bubbly personality and openness are helping him take it all in his stride.

'Yes. Your third chakra defends what you believe in, and because you don't really believe in anything you're doing with your work, your third chakra has "retired". Your fifth chakra has to do with your creative expression, which there's no opportunity for in your job, so it's also taken early retirement.'

Paul sighs. 'I started doing IT because I'm good at it and I needed a regular pay cheque. I was only going to do it for a few years so I could save some money to pursue my true loves – painting, writing and performing. That was ten years ago.'

'Yes, and now you've got a house with a mortgage and lots of other debt, leaving you with no way to finance your

dreams. You're also afraid that if you follow your heart, you'll lose the love and respect of your parents, who are proud of their "reliable" son and his "reliable" job. Paul, you've never even told them what you really want to do.'

'I know!' he says with such good humour that we both laugh.

'It's all okay,' I tell him. 'I'm going to show you how to get your chakras working so you can finally pursue the work you love.'

I explain the chakra balancing and cleansing that Paul can do to get his chakras strong and revitalised. As we're about to end the session, Paul interrupts me.

'Can I ask one more question?' he says sheepishly.

'Of course,' I say.

'I don't know how to tell my girlfriend I want to end our relationship. Do you have any advice?'

'Girlfriend?' I ask, and I'm driven to an uncharacteristic fit of giggles. Paul's second chakra clearly shows me that he's homosexual.

Paul laughs too, as I tell him what I see.

'Well, I guess I have some other things to work on too,' he says, and I know by his good-natured and open-minded disposition that he's going to be just fine.

Lisa

In this day and age (for most people) just getting a pay cheque isn't enough; loving and finding meaning in your work and having the right career matters. Sometimes people are convinced they are in a career that is right for them, but actually isn't. This is the case with Lisa. As soon as I hear her on the phone, I know she's experienced significant disappointment and despair. Her voice is thick with bitterness, and her energy field shows me she's been carrying a burden of sadness for many years.

'Lisa, I'm reading your energy field and I see in your fifth chakra that you have been gifted with an exceptional singing voice, but that this gift is also a source of despair for you. You've always wanted to become a professional singer, but haven't been able to achieve your dream.'

Lisa begins to cry. 'Yes,' she confirms.

'Early in your career you started having problems with your voice,' I continue. 'Sore throats, infections, strained vocal cords . . . You went to a number of specialists and no one could figure out why this kept happening to you.'

'Yes,' Lisa sniffs. 'I had to cancel so many singing jobs that I was labelled "unreliable", and no one wanted to book me anymore. My career ended before it even began.'

'And all this time you've felt like you lost out on your true calling.'

'Yes,' she says again, with deep anguish in her voice.

I can see forty-five years of accumulated despair and bitterness in Lisa's chakras. But I see something else as well. 'Lisa, you have an incredible teacher energy. Do you teach singing?'

'It pays the bills,' she says sourly. 'It's pathetic, isn't it? Here I am teaching other people how to fulfil my dream!'

209

'Here's the thing, Lisa,' I say. 'I know how badly you wanted to be a singer, but you truly are a gifted teacher. Your lack of recognition of this gift, and of the positive impact you have on your students' lives, is robbing you of the joy it could bring you.'

'But I was supposed to be a famous singer,' she protests, 'not some teacher!!'

'Maybe that's not true,' I counter. 'Maybe you are where you are supposed to be. What if all the time you spent training to be a singer was actually training you to be what you were meant to become all along – an extremely talented singing teacher? Sometimes it's not our circumstances that present problems in our lives, but rather our beliefs about them.' I say this not only to challenge Lisa, but also because it's what I genuinely see in her energy field. Her teacher energy is far stronger than her singer and performer energy. Sadly, she is so blinded by her bitterness at the loss of her singing career that she can't see the impact she makes as a teacher.

'Doesn't your heart fill with pride at hearing your students sing a song you taught them to sing?' I ask. 'Don't you love helping your students become great singers?'

'No,' she says flatly. 'Watching other people receive praise for their singing just drives the knife of loss deeper into my heart. It should be me out there. People should be looking at me and applauding me for my amazing voice.'

I see that Lisa's fifth chakra blockage is causing her physical discomfort in addition to her emotional baggage. Not only is she lonely and isolated, but she also has chronic neck and shoulder pain.

I tell her this, and explain that she can release her feelings of bitterness and heal from her physical pain if she commits to cleansing her chakras, with a special focus on chakra 5.

'Maybe it's just too late for me,' she says.

'Just give it a try,' I reply. Though she agrees to work on her chakras, as I hang up the phone, I am sceptical about whether she actually will.

Kellie

'So what can you tell me?' Kellie says, settling into the chair and looking at me expectantly. She's wearing a perfectly tailored pantsuit and designer heels, but what stands out most about her appearance is her bright red lipstick. And what stands out most in her energy field are significant blockages in her third and fifth chakras.

After going over the formalities about how the session will go, I start right in with what I see in her energy field. 'You're having trouble meeting the right man.'

'You can say that again,' she says, rolling her eyes. 'Every guy I meet turns out to be a jerk. But I guess I shouldn't be surprised – it takes a strong man to be with a strong woman.'

'"Strong" is one word for it, but I'm seeing something else,' I say. 'You've got blockages in your third and fifth chakras, and I'm seeing that you can be quite argumentative. You tend to be very fixed in your beliefs about what's right and wrong, and you aren't a good listener.'

'Sure, I know what's right and wrong,' she says. 'It's my job to teach others what's right and wrong. Really, they should thank me.'

'I'm seeing that you also like to be the boss in your relationships.'

'Like my mother used to say: It's my way or the highway. She didn't raise me to be a pushover. She said, "Kellie, you've got to stand up for yourself, otherwise you'll find yourself scurrying to have dinner on the table every night for some man you can barely stand." There's no way that's going to happen to me.' In reality, most of the men Kellie has dated aren't jerks at all, but rather nice guys who simply get fed up with her nastiness disguised as assertiveness, and her unwillingness to listen or compromise.

'Kellie,' I say, 'a healthy sense of self-esteem isn't about dominating others or making them bend to your will. It isn't about trying to make others believe what we believe. Rather, a person with healthy self-esteem feels so secure within themselves that they are happy to let others simply be.'

Kellie looks at me sceptically, but remains uncharacteristically quiet.

'I'm not telling you that you should be meek; it's good to know your mind. But imposing your will on others is really damaging your relationships. Are you open to trying something different?'

Kellie crosses her arms and sits for a minute. Finally, she nods. 'All right,' she says.

I'm not sure whether Kellie will follow my advice or whether her overenergised fifth chakra will draw her *back to her old ways, but I teach her the chakra cleansing practice and hope for the best.*

Allyson

I'm sitting in front of my computer, watching as a woman in her early thirties appears via Skype. 'Hi, Allyson,' I say. 'Are you ready for your session?'

'I'm so excited,' she says, clapping her hands together. 'Let's do it!'

As I'm explaining to Allyson how the session will go, I'm already getting impressions about her. I can see right away that she's recently launched a career as a life coach and intuitive. I see that she speaks to most of her clients via web calls like this one.

'How's your coaching going?' I ask her. In fact, I can see how it's going – slowly. But I'm interested to hear what Allyson has on her mind, because I also see in her energy field that what she thinks is the problem actually isn't.

'Wow, you can see that I'm a coach? That's amazing!' Allyson flashes a wide smile, but she's not nearly as confident as it implies.

'Yes, you started recently after finishing an online course.'

'That's right! I took time off work when my daughter was born and realised I didn't want to go back. One of my friends is a life coach and an intuitive, and she told me I should take this course her coach offers to figure out what I want to do. Turns out I'm meant to be a life coach too!'

'So you invested in headshots and a website and all your materials, but you're having trouble getting your business going,' I say. 'You've spent a lot of money on this course and on getting your branding in order, but you're not sure where to go from here.'

'Amazing,' she says. 'That's right. I just feel like there must be something blocking me from getting myself out there, you know? I've been reading about chakras and I think my throat chakra is weak or spinning backwards or something, otherwise I wouldn't be having problems getting myself noticed. What do you see?'

'I think one of your main challenges is time,' I say, prompting a quizzical expression from Allyson.

'You mean I'm not spending enough time developing my business?' she asks. 'I know my branding needs more work, but I'm doing a business booster seminar next week and —'

'That's not exactly what I mean,' I interrupt. 'From what I see, you've set off on this path of being a coach and an intuitive without any real experience. I can see that your natural intuitive abilities aren't very developed, and you haven't yet had the life or career experience to become a coach. In fact, I'm seeing that coaching is not a good choice for you. I do see some degree of imbalance in your fifth chakra, but what it's showing me is that you haven't yet surrendered to divine will; to the higher purpose of your life. You decided to become a coach because the opportunity presented itself and this school provided "a path to success". But coaching is not in line with your energy.'

Allyson's gone pale. I feel bad for her, but I wouldn't be doing her any favours by hiding the truth. 'What is in line with my energy?' she asks.

'I see you've got very strong creative energy, and you're very good at writing and art. At one point, you briefly considered writing down and illustrating the stories you make up for your daughter, but you pushed it aside as unrealistic.'

'It's amazing that you can see that! That's true!' she says.

'Yes, and I also see that being a children's book author and illustrator is something that appeals to you; it's definitely in line with your energy. Much more than being a life coach.'

'I was so sure about this coach thing, but I guess if I really listen to myself, you're right. In truth, I don't like working as a coach much. I did it because I thought it would be a good way to make money and be at home with my daughter.'

'I understand, Allyson, and please know you haven't done anything wrong. What we need to do now is get your chakras balanced so you're better able to develop and listen to your own intuition,' I say. 'Your intuition was trying to give you that message in the first place. That's why you know that what I'm telling you is true.'

'My husband's going to be upset. I just spent all that money on coaching.'

'I understand, but it's not a loss. You can use all the tools you learned to become a coach to get started with this other venture. In fact, you could become so successful that maybe one day you'll start a side business coaching other book writers and illustrators. When you truly surrender

your personal will to your soul's will, things have an interesting way of coming together.'

Allyson gives a nervous smile. 'Look,' I say, 'I understand that making money is a real concern. If you can go back to your old job, it could support you while you follow your creative path. And I have a hunch, call it a psychic one, that you can easily get your old job back.'

'Well,' she says, 'I did like that job. It's just that . . . Well, I thought it would be an easier schedule and I could make a lot more money being a coach. But, now that you mention it, I really don't love talking to all these people about their problems and struggles. I thought maybe it was because I'm not good at it yet, but I always get nervous for the calls and I don't know what to say. Do you honestly think I should give children's books a go?'

'If it resonates with you, which it seems to, then yes. Just start slow, then you won't be putting so much pressure on yourself to succeed immediately. It should be something you enjoy!'

'You know, as you're saying this, I feel all lit up – like something in me is coming alive for the first time!' Allyson's smile is back, and this time it's genuine.

Chakra 5 self-assessment

To get an idea of how fit and healthy your fifth chakra is, ask yourself the following questions:

Y / N Do I openly and honestly communicate how I feel/
believe?

Y / N   Do I speak up if I feel mistreated?

Y / N   Do I try to clear things up if I've been misunderstood or have misunderstood a situation?

Y / N   Do I express and act upon my creative ideas and inspirations?

Y / N   Do I listen to other people, do other people feel heard by me and do I allow others to have their own point of view?

Y / N   Am I open to all points of view and willing to grow and be challenged about what I believe?

Y / N   Am I respectful of other people's authentic self-expression?

Y / N   Can I objectively examine my own beliefs and acknowledge that I'm not always right?

Y / N   Do I have an outlet to express my authentic and individual self?

Y / N   Do I creatively express myself and 'sing my own soul song'?

Y / N   Am I free of neck, throat, jaw, teeth and/or thyroid problems?

If you answered 'no' to a few of these questions, you have some challenges with your fifth chakra. If you answered 'no' to many of them, you probably have a significant blockage.

Chakra 5 out of balance

If your fifth chakra is not working properly, you may have challenges with your physical or emotional health, finances, love life, relationships with family and friends or your career and creativity. Remember that an imbalance in one chakra will likely affect the energy flow to the chakras above and below it. So if you have a weak or blocked chakra 5 you may experience one or more of the problems related to chakras 1 to 4 too.

The following are some challenges you may experience if your fifth chakra is imbalanced.

Physical health
- ❖ Neck, jaw, teeth or tongue problems
- ❖ Sore throats, losing your voice, a weak voice or other vocal problems
- ❖ Thyroid/hormonal imbalances
- ❖ Gum problems or mouth ulcers
- ❖ Chronic cough
- ❖ Swollen glands, laryngitis or tonsillitis

Emotional health
- ❖ Shy, nervous, won't speak up, overly introverted
- ❖ Fear of public speaking and of being seen and heard
- ❖ Soft/weak voice
- ❖ 'Ghost-like' energy or demeanour
- ❖ Speaking difficulties, such as stuttering and pronunciation problems
- ❖ Brash, loud, aggressive, overly extroverted and attention-seeking
- ❖ Gossiping, talking too much and can't listen
- ❖ Dishonest or 'telling tales'
- ❖ Lack of will and decisiveness, not clear in your choices/actions
- ❖ Critical, judgemental or envious

Finances

- ❖ Don't have a job/career that fits your unique expression
- ❖ Crave to do/be what you love
- ❖ Difficulties getting what you want, aren't seen and/or heard
- ❖ Can't work as a team with others
- ❖ Can't put your unique stamp on things
- ❖ Can't tell the world what you want to say

Love life

- ❖ Communication issues including misunderstandings and frustrations
- ❖ Feel rejected and alienated
- ❖ Struggle to have a love relationship where your partner accepts who you are and what you want to do in the world

Relationships with friends and family

- ❖ Similar issues as with romantic relationships
- ❖ Communication issues including misunderstandings and frustrations
- ❖ Feel rejected and alienated

Career and creativity

- ❖ Communication issues
- ❖ Fear of speaking out, public speaking and honest and open conversations
- ❖ Writer's block
- ❖ Difficulty expressing your creativity
- ❖ Fear of expressing your individual self

Nourishing chakra 5

Among the activities and experiences your fifth chakra likes are:

- ❖ The colour blue
- ❖ Singing
- ❖ Public speaking
- ❖ Writing, acting and performing
- ❖ Speaking your truth
- ❖ Great discussions with interesting and like-minded people
- ❖ Any activity in which you feel you are expressing yourself

You probably won't be surprised to learn that among Paul, Lisa, Kellie and Allyson, there were mixed results.

Paul did well sticking to his chakra cleansing routine. When I spoke to him several months after his session, he was still working in IT but was painting again. In fact, he had even sold two of his paintings and was paying down his debt, as well as devising an exit strategy from his job. He was also doing some deep exploration into his sexuality, allowing himself to acknowledge feelings he'd long suppressed.

Sadly, when I spoke to Lisa, she was still in the same lonely and bitter space as before. She admitted to having tried the chakra cleanse once or twice, but said that she didn't see how it could possibly help her.

Kellie surprised me. When I spoke with her she said she'd been working consistently to balance her chakras. She reported that she felt calmer overall, and had begun to see how her previous aggression had hurt many of her relationships.

She was even thinking about taking her mother to a meditation class with her!

When I spoke to Allyson nearly a year after our session, she was perkier than ever. She had returned to her old job and had taken to the idea of children's books with gusto, writing down all her favourite stories. She planned to illustrate a mock-up of one of these stories for an upcoming conference where she'd have a chance to show it to some agents.

CHAPTER 26

CHAKRA 6: INTUITION

Chakra 6 is the sixth level of your energy anatomy. Also known as the third eye chakra, this is where you encounter your higher mind. Chakra 6 is located above and between your eyebrows, in the middle of your forehead.

In working on your fifth chakra, you began learning to express yourself originally and authentically, and to surrender your personal will, allowing yourself to hear the guidance of a higher consciousness. In working on chakra 6, you explore this higher consciousness further, expanding your awareness to what lies beyond the earth plane.

Chakra 6 rules your spirituality as well as your psychic abilities and intuition. This is the chakra to focus on when you seek to develop these aspects of your life, including opening the third eye.

Your sixth chakra is about transcendence, or going truly 'above and beyond' by opening yourself to real wisdom – the balance of imagination and intellect. An open and healthy sixth chakra allows a balance to be struck between the right (feminine/creative/imaginative) and left (masculine/organisational/intellect-based) sides of the brain. When your sixth chakra is strong and healthy, both of these sides of your brain work in partnership together. Then you can dream big things into being!

Chakra 6 basics

Names
Chakra 6 is also called the third eye chakra.

Location
It is located above and between the eyebrows.

Areas of body governed
This chakra oversees the physical areas of the head, including the brain (the hypothalamus, pituitary gland and pituitary nerve plexus), ears and eyes.

Drive and issues
Chakra 6 governs your ability to transcend this earth plane and to access wisdom.

Most people are weak in their sixth chakra, and this imbalance can play out in a variety of ways. Let's look at some clients I've worked with who have had blockages and other imbalances in chakra 6.

Case studies

Celia

Celia practically floats into the room. She's dressed all in white, with a long, sheer white top, billowy white pants and white sandals. She has the most serene expression on her face. Rather than sit down, she slides towards me.

'My friend, it is so good to see you again,' she says. 'The angels tell me we have known each other during several lifetimes. They told me to come see you and that you will tell me something life-changing.' She pulls me into a big hug. She seems genuine, though quite strange. She and I have not met before in this or any other lifetime. However, I don't want to be unprofessional, so I keep my thoughts to myself. I smile and kindly ask her to take a seat.

As I look at Celia's energy field, I'm struck by the massive imbalance between her higher and lower chakras. 'Right away, I'm seeing that chakras 6 and 7 are engorged, while your lower chakras, especially 1 to 3, are quite weak. I see you spend a lot of time in meditation, and you work as an intuitive,' I say. I can see in her energy field and just from looking at her that Celia is barely here. I almost feel like I need to tie a tether to her before she floats away! I have been seeing this more often lately. Many people are taking an increased interest in consciousness and spirituality, which is great, but often they don't understand the importance of having strong earthly chakras. Without these, you can't awaken the higher chakras.

'*Your lower chakras are showing me a disconnectedness from your body,*' *I say.* '*You're spending a lot of time and energy focusing on transcendence and listening to your guides, but what you're hearing as guidance isn't always accurate.*' *Her gauzy demeanour shifts.*

'*But I hear them clearly,*' *she says, obviously surprised by what I've said.*

'*I can see that you are more intuitive than most,*' *I reassure her,* '*yet what you perceive isn't always clear; the messages are sometimes garbled. This is due to an imbalance between the feminine and masculine sides of your brain – you're almost entirely in the feminine. It's the balance between feminine and masculine that increases intuitive abilities.*'

Celia smiles and her eyes again soften and mist over. '*It is the divine feminine working through me. The sisterhood is rising,*' *she declares.*

'*Yes,*' *I say,* '*that may be the case, but the feminine and masculine energies are of equal importance; their polarity is necessary for balance. In your case, your inability to engage your left brain is why you're struggling to take your business where you want it to go. You're praying for success and meditating on it, sage-smudging your home and workspace and doing positive affirmations, but you're not being as practical as you need to be to make your dreams a reality. You must also take time to devise and implement a plan to make it all happen.*'

'Hmm,' she says, contemplating what I've said.

'Also, it's important to understand that our guides and angels don't tell us what to do — that's not their role,' I explain. 'They may help us to see various elements of a situation, but they don't determine what choices are "right" or "wrong" for us. They support free will; you must make your own choices. Their real purpose is to help us learn from and integrate the lessons we encounter as a result of those choices here on earth.'

'Then who would you say is giving me this guidance?' she asks.

'It could be your ego . . . Sometimes what we think we hear as guidance is actually our ego encouraging us to do something in its interests.'

'Hmm,' she says again, nodding, taking it all in.

'Strengthening your lower chakras and working on that left–right brain balance will support your intuitive capabilities and help you distinguish your intuition from your ego,' I say. 'And speaking of strengthening the lower chakras, you would also benefit from physical exercise,' I continue. 'And you need to get off your meditation cushion and get outside and interact with nature,' I say. 'This will help you ground into your body and strengthen your lower chakras. You need to be in touch with the earth and feel the joy and delight of this earthly existence instead of trying to "bliss out" all the time.'

'Hmm,' she says again. 'I hear what you're saying, and I'm willing to explore it.'

'Good,' I say, and I show her how to balance her chakras.

Jacob

Frankly, I'm surprised Jacob has come to see me. As he sits before me in his button-down shirt, casual blue jeans and loafers, he seems relaxed and friendly, yet I can see in his energy field that he is highly sceptical of me. In fact, he thinks the entire field of medical intuition sounds like a bunch of woo-woo garbage.

'I understand how you feel,' I tell Jacob after I give him my introductory speech. 'I'm sceptical about many psychics and intuitives as well. And I'm also not into the woo-woo.'

He raises his eyebrows and I smile. 'I can see it in your energy field,' I say. 'I also see that you're here because your girlfriend told you to come.' Jacob looks slightly uneasy as he uncrosses then re-crosses his legs.

'I think it's healthy to be sceptical. That's one reason I didn't want you to tell me anything before I read your energy field — so you can have confidence that what I tell you is what I see. Now, let's get started and you can make up your mind for yourself.'

Jacob gives a nod and leans back into the chair.

'I see you've been having migraines for a long time now,' I begin. 'Since you were a child, in fact. That's going on thirty years. You used to get them only once in a while, but now you get them more frequently and it's starting to affect your work.' Jacob stares at me, poker-faced, and I continue. 'You've also started having anxiety attacks in the last few months, and this is causing you particular embarrassment.'

I pause, and though I'm not looking for confirmation – I can see all this in his energy field – Jacob does offer a small nod.

'I know you've been to a number of specialists, trying medications and even some alternative therapies, but nothing so far has helped. And I can see why. Now, stick with me, because I know how this is going to sound to you . . .' I tell him about the chakra system, explaining that chakras are energy vortexes that govern various areas of our lives, including our physical and emotional wellbeing. 'You've got a large blockage in your sixth chakra, and that's what's causing your headaches and anxiety.' As I anticipated, Jacob sighs and gives me a 'you've got to be kidding' look.

I smile. 'I understand this doesn't fit with how you see the world. You're analytical. You want facts and proof, but this is also binding up your throat and heart chakras. You are trying to tightly control your life and exert your will in it rather than listening to divine will, and you are not communicating your feelings and letting love flow freely in your life. This in turn is causing problems in your relationship. You don't allow yourself to love or express yourself openly. Your girlfriend feels you are withholding. You also have a wonderfully creative side to your personality, yet you don't let yourself explore it because you don't value it. I see that you used to love putting on plays as a child.'

Now I've struck a chord. 'How do you know that? My girlfriend doesn't even know that.'

'Like I said, it's here in your energy field . . . Jacob, you've got to learn to embrace your intuitive and creative

229

side – that's what's bringing on these headaches and anxiety attacks. You're actually highly intuitive, but you suppress it. When you were a child, you used to see and feel all kinds of things about people, but when you told your parents, they told you you were making it up. They looked at you as if you were strange, and that hurt so much you shut that part of yourself down. Most of us start shutting down our natural intuitive abilities in childhood because adults discourage this kind of thing. In your case, the judgement placed on you caused you to become so judgemental of creative and visionary types that you sought the opposite path and went into a field where you could be surrounded by the certainty of numbers.'

Jacob is speechless for several minutes. I know I've given him a lot to process, so I allow him space to sit with what I've said.

'My girlfriend says I act like a robot sometimes, but . . .' he pauses. 'I have feelings, I just . . . I don't know how to express them.'

'I understand. You've numbed yourself to a lot of what you felt as a child, and it's difficult to undo that. But it's possible. It will take work, but you can learn to open those parts of yourself again in a way that feels safe. All your chakras could use some love and attention, Jacob. Are you willing to put your scepticism aside for a bit and try?'

'Will this make my headaches go away?' he asks.

'It may take time, but yes, I believe it will, if you meditate and dedicate yourself to a regular chakra balancing practice.'

'Ugh.' Jacob rolls his eyes. 'My girlfriend won't let me hear the end of it; she's been trying to get me to do meditation for years,' he says, but his tone is soft.

'This is the thing, Jacob. You shut yourself down because you're such a sensitive person, but this has led to you functioning only in your left brain – the analytical side. The chakra work will help you create a healthy balance between left and right, bringing in more of that creative and emotional side, and making a safe space for those aspects of yourself you've been hiding.'

'All right,' he says, 'I'll give it a try, but only because I feel like I can trust you.'

'See?' I say, 'you're already starting to listen to your intuition!'

Arthur

Arthur is an adorable older gentleman who has come to me because his wife was thrilled with the work she and I had done together. He's been doing my *Chakra Cleanse Meditation*, but he's contacted me saying he still feels 'absolutely nothing'.

At first I'm not surprised; some people don't feel the effects of the chakra balancing and cleansing immediately. After a few weeks, however, Arthur tells me things haven't improved, so we've set up a telephone call to get to the bottom of this.

I can't help but smile at this sweet man; I get such a clear psychic impression of his appearance, with his downy *white hair and glowing eyes. He's such a kind person, with a delightful enthusiasm, and he really wants to become more spiritually aware. When I look at Arthur's energy field, I see that his sixth chakra is tiny. 'Arthur,' I say, 'it looks like your sixth chakra is sleeping!'*

'Well, how do we wake it up?' he says, nearly shouting, and we both laugh.

'We just need to do some focused training to help enliven it.' I assure him that in no time at all he'll start feeling intuitive hunches.

'Great! Then maybe I'll start playing the lottery!' he jokes. We laugh again. 'The sixth chakra opens you up to the world beyond that which you knew previously existed,' I continue. 'After this, your energy will begin to move to the seventh chakra and here, you'll begin to experience the bliss of knowing you are one with all that is.'

'All right,' Arthur says, rubbing his hands together expectantly. 'Let's get started!'

Lara

Lara comes to me after having attended one of my lectures at a spirituality conference. She sits cross-legged in the chair opposite me. She's a pleasant young woman with dark, braided hair, wearing a peasant blouse and jeans. What stands out most about her appearance, however, are the brightly coloured temporary tattoos of ornate symbols that adorn her chest and arms.

So far in the session, I've read her energy field and provided her with some advice for balancing her under-active first and second chakras.

'Now I'll answer any questions you have,' I say.

'Here's the thing,' she says, leaning forward in the chair. 'Ever since I saw you at the conference, I've known that I want to be psychic! I just know working as an intuitive is my soul purpose.' Her eyes are dancing as she speaks. 'I want to have visions and be able to read people's energy fields, just like you can.'

I smile and nod. Over the years, many people have asked me how they can become psychic or 'like me'. I tell Lara what I've told them.

'I think it's wonderful that you want to develop your psychic abilities, but I feel I must caution you. Being extremely psychic and empathic is more complicated than it appears and is more labour-intensive,' I say. 'It's a lot to manage. Even with the years of work I've done on my chakras to help balance my abilities and keep healthy boundaries, it's still a work in progress. I have to admit there are some days when I wish I wasn't so psychic . . . that it would just all go away. It's also important to understand that each of us is unique. It's not possible for you or anyone else to be just like me or any other psychic or intuitive.'

Lara's expression falls slightly.

'However,' I say quickly, 'that doesn't mean you can't develop some kind of psychic or empathic abilities. Just keep in mind that there are many different kinds of sensing. Clairvoyance, or "clear seeing", is only one.

When you develop your abilities, you could be clairaudient or clairsentient, or a combination.'

'Okay!' She brightens up again. 'How do I do it?'

'It takes time to develop these abilities,' I say. 'You have to build yourself up to it. A sudden massive psychic opening would throw you into an imbalance and could even be dangerous.'

I show her how to do the Chakra Cleanse Meditation. 'If you do this regularly it will energise chakras 1–5, and when you're ready, chakras 6 and 7 will start to open up. Over time, you'll likely notice an increase in your psychic abilities.'

'Cool!' Lara says, grinning.

Chakra 6 self-assessment

To get an idea of how fit and healthy your sixth chakra is, ask yourself the following questions:

Y / N Am I intuitive, and do I follow intuitive hunches?

Y / N Do I use my intellect as well as my intuition? Am I balanced between my left and right brain?

Y / N Can I visualise? Can I envision my ideal life?

Y / N Do I use my imagination? Do I dream, daydream or see images and stories in my mind?

Y / N Am I aware of my negative programming, of how the visionary side of me has been discouraged?

Y / N Do I have a high degree of self-awareness?

Y / N Have I had psychic/intuitive experiences? Have I had visions, premonitions or feelings (including sensory experiences) about something that have proved to be accurate?

Y / N Am I free of headaches, migraines, nightmares and brain, eye or ear problems?

If you answered 'no' to a few of these questions, you have some challenges with your sixth chakra. If you answered 'no' to many of them, you probably have a significant blockage.

Chakra 6 out of balance

If your sixth chakra is not working properly, you may have problems with your physical or emotional health, finances, love life, relationships with family and friends or your career and creativity. Again, remember that an imbalance in one chakra will likely affect the energy flow to the chakras above and below it. So if you have a weak or blocked chakra 6 you may experience one or more of the problems related to chakras 1 to 5 as well.

You might experience some of the following challenges if your sixth chakra is imbalanced.

Physical health
* Sinus or nasal problems
* Eye problems
* Headaches or migraines
* Some neurological disturbances

Emotional health
* Lack wisdom or self-perception
* Lack 'vision', can't see possibilities
* Can't focus, concentrate, visualise or imagine

- ❖ Can't be intuitive and see/hear/feel/communicate with energy/spiritual worlds
- ❖ Can't remember your dreams
- ❖ Limited thinking, can't reprogram yourself
- ❖ Left and right brain hemispheres aren't balanced
- ❖ Deluded
- ❖ 'All up in your head' and not grounded in reality

Finances
- ❖ Lack insight about what is blocking your financial flow
- ❖ Lack insight about how to make money
- ❖ Won't dare step into the unlimited possibilities and create what you desire
- ❖ Can't focus and concentrate

Love life
- ❖ Closed-minded
- ❖ Live in a fantasy world, not grounded
- ❖ Not able to self-evaluate, or resist self-evaluation
- ❖ Feelings of being inadequate
- ❖ Don't learn from your mistakes
- ❖ Lack vision or scope for your relationship

Relationships with friends and family
- ❖ Similar problems as with love life
- ❖ Can't understand people/social cues

Career and creativity
- ❖ Lack vision
- ❖ Lack perspective

❖ Can't take career or creativity to great heights
❖ Poor memory
❖ Struggle with focus

Nourishing chakra 6

In addition to the Chakra Cleanse Meditation, the things your sixth chakra likes include:

❖ The colour indigo
❖ Meditation
❖ Visualisation
❖ Brainstorming and goal-setting
❖ Mastermind groups
❖ Consciously dreaming your ideal life
❖ Any activities that inspire you to stretch yourself and be great

What about Celia, Jacob, Arthur and Lara?

When I spoke with Celia several months later, I was happy to hear she'd taken what I said to heart. In addition to doing the chakra balancing, she had started a tai chi practice, which helped her feel more grounded in her body and got her outdoors more often. She still had work to do, but she had definitely made progress. She had also stopped asking her guides and angels for advice on all her decisions, and had learned instead to use the increased clarity of her intuition to guide her.

Jacob initially had trouble with the chakra balancing and meditation; he had to work to get beyond his scepticism. But he eventually tried it, and after several weeks, his migraines and anxiety attacks did begin to abate. He was also slowly opening up to the idea of revisiting aspects of himself such as the deeply caring and intuitive nature he'd suppressed since childhood.

To Arthur's excitement, it only took a couple of sessions for his sixth chakra to respond. Now he and his wife can both talk about what they experience when they work on their chakras.

Five months after her session, Lara approached me after another lecture, when I was chatting with members of the audience. To her credit, she'd persisted with the Chakra Cleanse Meditation. She told me that while she hadn't developed the ability to have visions about the future as she'd hoped, she had started to sense things about people and situations, and was delighted that, increasingly, the things she sensed were confirmed to be true. 'I'm doing it!' She smiled and threw her arms around me, giving me an enthusiastic hug.

CHAPTER 27

CHAKRA 7: ENLIGHTENMENT

Chakra 7 is the seventh level of your energy anatomy. Also called the crown chakra, chakra 7 is located at the top of the head. This is the chakra where you experience enlightenment.

In chakras 5 and 6, you begin the process of surrendering to the divine. This process is fully realised in chakra 7.

By truly merging with divinity, we experience oneness with all that is. When you 'surrender to the universe', you commit an act of radical transformative power – you allow divinity to express itself through you. You then start to live your life based on this alignment with your higher path or calling.

Your seventh chakra enables you to feel true interconnectedness and enlightenment. Experiencing this allows you to trust in the universe. When you stop believing in the idea of your separateness, which is a creation of the ego, you lose your fear. Instead, you trust and know that you are one with all that is.

Chakra 7 basics

Names
Chakra 7 is also called the crown chakra.

Location
It is located on the top of the head.

Areas of body governed
This chakra oversees the physical areas of the upper brain and nervous system.

Drive and issues
Chakra 7 governs your ability to feel a sense of oneness with the universe and to surrender to divinity.

Just as most people are weak in their sixth chakra, many also have challenges with chakra 7. Many of my clients have had blockages and other imbalances in their seventh chakra. Let's look at a few of them.

Case studies

Terry

Before we even begin our session, I can see that Terry feels like an outsider; as if she's unseen by anyone and somehow exists all alone, separate and outside the realm of the divine. We're Skyping, and as she sits there in a cosy sweater in front of a roaring fire, I can see the sadness in her energy field.

'You carry a deep sense of loneliness because you feel you've been trying to make a connection with the universe, but you don't feel that anyone's speaking back to you. You want desperately to feel that peace and connectedness, but you're struggling to get there,' I say. 'You've read lots of books about spirituality, and you even attend a consciousness-raising group, but the problem is that you're trying to understand the universe and divinity through your mind. There's very much an experiential as well as emotional component to opening yourself to divine connection. You have to "feel" love and divinity. That's how you can know love and divinity.'

'That's what they told me in the group,' she says. 'But how do I do that?'

'By doing things such as meditating and allowing yourself to connect deeply with nature; things that evoke the experience of "feeling" the divine,' I say. 'And by letting it happen in its own time. You can't rush these things.'

I go on. 'Your lower chakras are very weak, so you're having trouble passing energy up through them to your higher chakras. Strengthening the lower chakras supports this passage of energy. When energy flows properly to the higher chakras you're then capable of having that experience of connecting to the divine. I can't emphasise this enough — it's critical to work from the bottom up to create balance and open the path to connectedness.'

Terry nods and chews her lower lip as she contemplates what I've said.

'I also see you're having issues with your back and digestive system,' I say. 'Balancing the lower chakras should help sort out these problems as well.'

'Oh well, that's good news,' Terry says, offering a slight smile. I can see that she is afraid. She wants to believe what I'm saying, but she has struggled with this for so long that she wonders if she's capable of doing what I suggest. I explain the chakra balancing and cleansing practice to her and try to reassure her that she's not beyond hope — far from it! She's a warm, kind person; she needs to start trusting herself, strengthening her lower chakras and allowing herself to be open to the experience of oneness.

Samuel / Adam

Samuel contacted me because he is deeply concerned about his son, Adam. He asks if I can read his son's energy field through him. I tell him I can, but will do so only if his son grants me permission, and if Samuel agrees not to tell me beforehand why he's worried about his son.

Adam consents, so Samuel and I set up the call. I get a strong psychic image of Samuel as a grey-haired and balding man with a kind face. His brow is furrowed with worry — and for good reason. I can see through him that something is very wrong with Adam's energy field.

Right away I see that there is almost no energy in Adam's lowest three chakras, and chakras 6 and 7 look enormous and distorted. They appear blown out, with the lower chakras buckling under the weight of the massive, overfilled higher chakras. Adam is completely ungrounded and has lost touch with reality.

What I see shocks me, and I gasp. 'What happened to him?' I'm so concerned I go against my rule of receiving no information from the client in advance. I have never before seen this degree of imbalance! Samuel tells me that it started when his son began attending a meditation and psychic development group. One evening after the group, Adam came home talking about all the 'different lights and colours' he could see around people. The next morning, he wouldn't get out of bed. Since then, he has suffered from frequent panic attacks, migraines and nightmares.

I ask Samuel what type of meditation practices his son has done, but he's not sure. All he knows is that Adam talked about how his teacher could make people psychic.

The pieces of the puzzle quickly fall into place for me. Adam's teacher showed Adam how to raise his energy quickly into chakras 6 and 7 so that he could become psychic. I tell Samuel this. 'Adam's five lower chakras were not yet strong enough. His energy field couldn't deal with the amount of energy surging into his higher chakras, so Adam suffered a "blowout", which has made him unstable.'

Samuel sounds both horrified and heartbroken. 'Can you help him?' he asks, his voice filled with desperation.

I know that chakra balancing will help Adam tremendously. What happened to him reminds me of what

I experienced when I was exorcised. I experienced a massive tear in my energy field and chakric imbalance as a result.

'Adam has suffered some psychic damage,' I say, 'but it is possible to correct it.' I explain the chakra balancing technique to Samuel. 'Do you think you can teach him how to do this, and monitor and gently remind him to keep doing it?' I ask.

Samuel agrees. 'Yes, anything to help him. His mother and I are worried sick.'

'Just have Adam keep with the program. You should see a turnaround before long,' I reassure him.

Jerome

Jerome is a metalworker. As he sits in front of me in his checked shirt and jeans, slouched and looking bored, I know he would probably rather be anywhere but here. I can see that he's here because his wife has sent him.

I explain to Jerome how the session will work, and he simply shrugs.

When I look at Jerome's energy field, what stands out are very underactive chakras 6 and 7, which is causing chronic insomnia. 'I see you have trouble sleeping, and this has been a problem for you for years,' I say.

Jerome stares at me.

'You're also feeling stiff and sore, making it difficult to do your job as it's so physical,' I continue. 'I can see you eat quite a lot of meat. Among other effects, this raises the acid level in the body, which is one reason you feel so stiff.

Your body's energy system doesn't cope well with a high meat intake, nor does it respond well to caffeine, sugar or alcohol or other drugs. Many people are also sensitive to grains.'

Jerome continues to stare, and I can't help but think that his wife probably has her hands full if she's trying to change his diet. I continue with the reading, telling Jerome about various other physical and emotional challenges. Finally, I explain the chakra system and how these physical and emotional issues link to challenges in his energy system.

'Your seventh chakra is concerned with your spirituality,' I explain to the expressionless Jerome, 'but beyond this, when chakra 7 is open and energy can move through it easily, your brain waves are nourished. This has a positive impact on your sleep. Your weak seventh chakra is why you have insomnia; your brain waves aren't being nourished.'

Jerome crosses his arms in front of his chest.

'Now that I've read your energy field,' I say, 'do you have any questions?'

'No,' he says, then looks at the clock, and back at me.

I explain to Jerome how he can balance his chakras. At the end of the session, he's perfectly polite; he stands and shakes my hand and thanks me for my time. I tell Jerome I'll send him an audio recording of the session in case he wants to listen again to what I've told him. He shrugs and walks out.

Chakra 7 self-assessment

To get an idea of how fit and healthy your seventh chakra is, ask yourself the following questions:

Y / N   Have I glimpsed enlightenment, the state of totality, bliss and oneness with all that is?

Y / N   Do I know I am consciousness, above and beyond the mind and its polarities?

Y / N   Do I feel deeply connected to the universe and divinity?

Y / N   Can I sit quietly without the need to think or do something? Can I simply be?

Y / N   Is my energy mostly rooted in the present moment? Can I meditate easily?

Y / N   Do I have an inkling of my soul purpose?

If you answered 'no' to a few of these questions, you have some challenges with your seventh chakra. If you answered 'no' to many of them (as most people do), you probably have a significant blockage.

Chakra 7 out of balance

If your seventh chakra is not working properly, you may have problems with your physical or emotional health, finances, love life, relationships with family and friends or your career and creativity. Remember that an imbalance in one chakra will likely affect the energy flow to the chakras above and below it. So if you have a weak or blocked chakra 7 you may experience one or more of the problems related to chakras 1 to 6 as well.

The following are challenges you could experience if your seventh chakra is imbalanced:

Physical health
❖ Migraines or headaches
❖ Brain problems

- ❖ Scalp or upper head issues
- ❖ Vertigo
- ❖ Hypersensitive in the extreme
- ❖ Chronic tiredness
- ❖ Hopelessness or depression

Emotional health

- ❖ Lack faith, trust, aren't 'spiritual'
- ❖ Can't still the mind or be still
- ❖ Lack purpose, orientation, don't know what you are here to do
- ❖ Confusion, escapism or delusions

Finances

- ❖ Lacking in faith and trust, living in fear
- ❖ Always hurrying to get somewhere or stressed about completing tasks
- ❖ Haven't begun to understand your life purpose, which has a dampening effect on your career

Love life

- ❖ Can't see that we are all one and interconnected, and can't connect with others
- ❖ Lack a humanitarian spirit

Relationships with friends and family

- ❖ Similar problems as with love life
- ❖ Can't see that we are all one and interconnected, and can't connect with others
- ❖ Lack a humanitarian spirit

Career and creativity

❖ Creative blocks
❖ Lack of understanding that you have a life purpose, or what that purpose is

Nourishing chakra 7

The following are things your seventh chakra likes:

❖ The colour violet
❖ Meditation, meditation and more meditation!
❖ Periods of stillness and reflection
❖ Books about saints, yogis and the great women and men of the world

What about Terry, Samuel's son Adam and Jerome?

When I checked in with Terry, right away I could tell she had more joy in her life. She confirmed that she wasn't feeling so despondent, and that she'd started meditating regularly and working on her chakras. While she hadn't yet had the dramatic enlightened moment she was hoping for (I reassured her that everyone experiences things differently), she was starting to have glimmers of something that felt like oneness.

When I spoke to Samuel again, his energy field showed a different man; he was much happier, and so was his son! He told me that just a few weeks after starting the chakra balancing exercises, Adam began to make a steady turnaround and was now back to his old, cheery self.

Several weeks after my session with Jerome, his wife called to tell me that she and their children had listened to the recording I'd sent him of our session. She said they laughed for hours afterwards because my description of him and his behaviour had been so accurate, despite him being so noncommittal. The session details also helped her finally understand some of the core reasons for Jerome's behaviour. Unfortunately, Jerome refused to do the chakra balancing or listen to the session again, but his wife said she would keep encouraging him.

CHAPTER 28

CHAKRA BALANCING AND THE CHAKRA CLEANSE MEDITATION

You now have a basic understanding of chakras 1 to 7; the aspects of your life and body that they govern, as well as the imbalances and problems blocked chakras can cause. However, in order to change your energy and change your life, it is important to also understand how these chakras work as a system. Once you grasp this, you'll be ready to start my Chakra Cleanse Meditation – a proven meditation I developed to heal, cleanse and strengthen your chakras.

Your lower, higher and cosmic chakras

Only when our five lower chakras (chakras 1 to 5) are strong and free of blockages and stagnation can we heal our shadow, embrace our light and pursue our soul purpose.

If you live in survival mode and struggle because of weak or blocked lower chakras, you won't have the time or resources

251

to focus on your soul purpose. Think about it: If you live from pay cheque to pay cheque, suffer from a health condition or don't have help and support in your life, you'll find it difficult to pursue your talents or passions.

Without strong lower chakras, you simply can't manifest your dreams. Further, if your lower chakras are weak or blocked, energy isn't passed up into your higher chakras, which is where your spiritual evolution takes place.

When you cleanse, balance and strengthen your lower chakras, you enable the energy to rise easily and steadily into your spiritual chakras: chakras 6 and 7. Your third eye and crown chakras play an important role in your life because they awaken you to your spiritual and mystical path.

When chakras 6 and 7 come alive and are energised, they act as a bridge to allow your energy to freely pass even higher – to your cosmic chakras – unlocking the path to understanding your soul purpose.

Chakras 8 to 12 are your cosmic chakras, completing your energetic system. With your five lower chakras healed and your two spiritual chakras activated, your energy then naturally rises into chakra 8 and you begin to discover your soul purpose for coming here in this lifetime.

Each one of us needs to develop a strong energetic structure within our energy fields to lift us up into the very high vibration of chakra 8 and that of chakras 9, 10, 11 and 12. As we rise into our higher chakras, we get closer to our soul purpose.

Practising the Chakra Cleanse Meditation to channel pure light through the lower seven chakras will help cleanse and balance your chakras, heal your shadow, find your light and understand your soul purpose.

Chakra balancing

The Chakra Cleanse Meditation presented in this chapter heals your chakras and your life by strengthening your lower five chakras (1 to 5). It also activates your spiritual chakras (6 and 7), helping you unlock and discover your intuitive talents and abilities, and it ignites your five higher cosmic chakras (8 to 12) as well. That's it – one meditation, done consistently, does all of this!

This meditation is tested and proven – it's a method I spent years developing (and adjusting). It's based upon what I could see in the energy fields of the people doing it. As a result, I am confident that if you do this meditation on a regular basis, you will see dramatic, positive changes in your life.

Ideally, you would do this chakra cleanse every day. But if you are new to meditation, aim to do it two to three times a week. Even if you do it only a few times a week, within months you'll have healed many parts of your life. Some people see major changes after just a few weeks.

How does the chakra cleanse work?

The Chakra Cleanse Meditation works in the following way: First, through the meditation, you enliven and open each of your lower chakras, starting with chakra 1 and going up to chakra 7. Second, you 'ignite the energy' of your five higher cosmic chakras by channelling the pure light down from your cosmic chakras into chakra 7, and on through to chakra 1.

To enliven and open each of the lower chakras, the meditation guides you to focus on the *point* – the physical location – of the chakra. First you focus on chakra 1, then 2, and so on. Then, once chakra 7 is open, the meditation guides you in allowing the pure light to flow downward. It's really that easy. Our energy system is designed in such a way that by simply focusing on the physical point of the chakra, it opens, energises and balances itself!

Getting started with chakra cleansing

Before you get started with cleansing and balancing your chakras, there are a few important things to note.

The Chakra Cleanse Meditation takes approximately forty-five minutes to complete, and it's important to do the entire meditation. You need to properly cleanse and balance all twelve chakras, as well as bring the pure light down into each chakra, for the meditation to be fully effective.

I realise that forty-five minutes might sound like a long time if you're new to meditation. Please don't panic! If you can only do the Chakra Cleanse Meditation once or twice a week at first, that's great – do that! Soon, you'll find it easy to stay restful and focused and, before you know it, you'll be doing it many more times a week and, eventually, every day.

Do the meditation in a place where you can relax and not be disturbed. This may sound obvious, but in our culture of busyness and multitasking, it's important to mention. Don't try to do it while checking messages on your phone, driving, or answering your children's questions.

It's up to you when you do the meditation; there is no

optimal time of day. Some prefer to make it part of their morning routine, others practise later at night when everyone else has gone to bed. Some even do it on their lunch break. The most important thing is to find the time when you are most likely to sit down and do it.

Another important point has to do with how you work with the chakras. Focusing on the point of each chakra is the primary practice, but as you read through the script for the meditation, you'll notice that I also mention the colour of each chakra. The most powerful way of opening and cleansing the chakras is to hold your awareness on each chakra point – being able to visualise the colour is secondary. So if you have trouble visualising the chakra colours – and many people do, though others find it can assist this process – simply skip this part of the meditation. You don't need to visualise the chakra colours for the meditation to be effective.

People often ask me if they need to visualise the chakras spinning, or opening up, or being filled with the pure light in order for the meditation to work properly, and the answer is no. If this naturally occurs while you hold your awareness on the chakra point, that's fine. Let it happen and flow with it. But don't worry about visualising anything beyond the point of each chakra. Once you bring your awareness to each chakra point and the chakras open themselves, you'll then be able to bring down the pure light easily and effectively.

The Chakra Cleanse Meditation

Without further ado, here is the Chakra Cleanse Meditation. This is the full transcript of the professionally recorded guided meditation available from my website. To purchase

the popular and much-loved guided version, please visit:
www.belindadavidson.com/store/

Begin now, by allowing your body to relax.

Breathe in . . . and out . . . Breathe in . . . and out . . .

Take a deep breath in . . . and gently breathe out the tension in your body . . .

Breathe in . . . and out . . . and relax your muscles totally, allowing your breath to flow gently and softly out your nose.

Take a deep breath in, breathing in relaxation . . . and release the breath, breathing out any remaining tension.

Draw your awareness now to your lower abdomen and pelvic region. This is where your first chakra is located. The colour of this chakra is red.

You begin to cleanse your first chakra by holding your focus on your lower abdomen and pelvis area.

As you breathe in and out, smoothly and softly, hold your point of focus on the first chakra.

As I begin to count from one to ten, you will continue to hold your focus on the area of your lower abdomen and pelvis . . . one, two, three, four, five, you hold your focus steady on the point of the first chakra while I continue to count, six, seven, eight, nine and ten.

Visualise the colour red, red like a red rose, or a strawberry or a raspberry. Imagine the colour red beginning to flow into your first chakra.

With every in-breath, visualise the colour red flowing into and filling up your first chakra . . . and with every out-breath, allow yourself to let go.

Breathe in, and as you do, you see red flowing in and filling up your first chakra . . . and as you breathe out, allow yourself to let go . . .

Practise this now a few times in your own time . . .

Draw your awareness now to just below your navel. This is where your second chakra is located. The colour of this chakra is orange.

You begin to cleanse your second chakra by holding your focus on the area just below your navel.

As you breathe in and out, smoothly and softly, hold your point of focus on the second chakra.

As I begin to count from one to ten, you will continue to hold your focus on the area just below your navel . . . one, two, three, four, five, you hold your focus steady on the point of the second chakra while I continue to count, six, seven, eight, nine and ten.

Visualise the colour orange, orange like the setting sun or perhaps of an orange.

With every in-breath, visualise the colour orange flowing into and filling up your second chakra . . . and with every out-breath allow yourself to let go.

Breathe in, and as you do, you see orange flowing in and filling up your second chakra . . . and as you breathe out, allow yourself to let go . . .

Practise this now a few times in your own time . . .

Draw your awareness to your stomach and solar plexus area. This is where your third chakra is located. The colour of this chakra is yellow.

You begin to cleanse your third chakra by holding your focus on your stomach area.

As you breathe in and out, smoothly and softly, hold your point of focus on the third chakra.

As I begin to count from one to ten, you will continue to hold your focus on the area of your stomach and solar plexus . . . one, two, three, four, five, you hold your focus steady on the point of the third chakra while I continue to count, six, seven, eight, nine and ten.

Visualise the colour yellow, yellow like the sun or a sunflower.

With every in-breath, visualise the colour yellow flowing into and filling up your third chakra . . . and with every out-breath allow yourself to let go.

Breathe in, and as you do, you see yellow flowing in and filling up your third chakra . . . and as you breathe out, allow yourself to let go . . .

Practise this now a few times in your own time . . .

Draw your awareness now to your heart region. This is where your fourth chakra is located. The colour of this chakra is green.

You begin to cleanse your fourth chakra by holding your focus on the area of your heart.

As you breathe in and out, smoothly and softly, hold your point of focus on the fourth chakra.

As I begin to count from one to ten, you will continue to hold your focus on the area of your heart region . . . one, two, three, four, five, you hold your focus steady on the point of the fourth chakra while I continue to count, six, seven, eight, nine and ten.

Visualise the colour green, green like rolling hills, or trees in a forest.

With every in-breath, visualise the colour green flowing into and filling up your fourth chakra . . . and with every out-breath allow yourself to let go.

Breathe in, and as you do, you see green flowing in and filling up your fourth chakra . . . and as you breathe out, allow yourself to let go . . .

Practise this now a few times in your own time . . .

Draw your awareness now to your throat. This is where your fifth chakra is located. The colour of this chakra is blue.

You begin to cleanse your fifth chakra by holding your focus on the area of your throat.

As you breathe in and out, smoothly and softly, hold your point of focus on the fifth chakra.

As I begin to count from one to ten, you will continue to hold your focus on your throat . . . one, two, three, four, five, you hold your focus steady on the point of the fifth chakra while I continue to count, six, seven, eight, nine and ten.

Visualise the colour blue, blue like the sky, or the ocean. With every in-breath, visualise the colour blue flowing into and filling up your fifth chakra . . . and with every out-breath allow yourself to let go.

Breathe in, and as you do, you see blue flowing in and filling up your fifth chakra . . . and as you breathe out, allow yourself to let go . . .

Practise this now a few times in your own time . . .

Draw your awareness to your third eye. Your third eye is located in the middle of your forehead, directly above the top of your nose. This is where your sixth chakra is located. The colour of this chakra is indigo.

You begin to cleanse your sixth chakra by holding your focus on your third eye.

As you breathe in and out, smoothly and softly, hold your point of focus on the sixth chakra.

As I begin to count from one to ten, you will continue to hold your focus on the area of your third eye . . . one, two, three, four, five, you hold your focus steady on the point of the sixth chakra while I continue to count, six, seven, eight, nine and ten.

Visualise the colour indigo. Indigo is a dark blue purplish colour. Indigo is the colour of a clear night sky.

Imagine the colour indigo beginning to flow into your sixth chakra.

With every in-breath, visualise indigo flowing into and filling up your sixth chakra . . . and with every out-breath allow yourself to let go.

Breathe in, and as you do, you see indigo flowing in and filling up your sixth chakra . . . and as you breathe out, allow yourself to let go . . .

Practise this now a few times in your own time . . .

Draw your awareness to the top of your head. This is where your seventh chakra is located. The colour of this chakra is violet.

You begin to cleanse your seventh chakra by holding your focus on the top of your head.

As you breathe in and out, smoothly and softly, hold your point of focus on the seventh chakra.

As I begin to count from one to ten, you will continue to hold your focus on the area of the top of your head . . .

one, two, three, four, five, you hold your focus steady on the point of the seventh chakra while I continue to count, six, seven, eight, nine and ten.

Visualise the colour violet, violet like lavender or grapes. With every in-breath, visualise the colour violet flowing into and filling up your seventh chakra . . . and with every out-breath allow yourself to let go.

Breathe in, and as you do, you see violet flowing in and filling up your seventh chakra . . . and as you breathe out, allow yourself to let go . . .

Practise this now a few times in your own time . . .

Your awareness moves to the area above your head, above where your seventh chakra is located. Chakras 8, 9, 10, 11 and 12 are located above the head and they ascend, starting at chakra 8 and ending with chakra 12, into the heavens.

Breathe in and out.

. . . and now, breathe in again . . . and out.

Draw your awareness again to above the top of your head, and hold your awareness there while I count . . . one, two, three, four, five, you hold your focus steady on the area of the higher five chakras while I continue to count, six, seven, eight, nine and ten.

Visualise a white light. The whitest and most brilliant light you can possibly imagine. Hold this image in your mind's eye for a few moments . . .

Now, visualise a funnel sitting on the top of your head . . . Visualise white light pouring into this funnel. Hold this image in your mind's eye for a few moments, and remember to keep breathing deeply, gently and evenly while you do this.

You now see white light pouring into your body through the funnel on the top of your head. You can feel this pure light filling up each of your chakras as it descends towards your feet.

You can feel the light pouring into your seventh chakra . . . and into your sixth chakra.

Breathe in and out . . . and feel how the pure light is pouring into your fifth chakra . . . and it's now moving down past your throat into your heart, filling up your heart chakra with pure light.

Breathe in and out . . . you feel the pure light moving down from your heart into your solar plexus, filling up your solar plexus with light.

Breathe in and out . . . and as you do, feel the pure light moving down from your solar plexus into your belly and abdomen, filling it up with light.

The energy is moving down to your pelvis and lower abdomen, filling them up too . . .

Breathe in and out . . . and feel the pure light moving down both of your legs, over your hips, over your knees, over your ankles, over your feet and down into the earth. You see the pure light going deep, down into the earth, grounding you with the earth.

All of your twelve chakras are now completely cleansed and balanced. Well done.

CONCLUSION

Thank you for sharing my journey so far. Being born too psychic felt like a curse, especially in my childhood. Only as an adult, when I learnt to balance my chakras, was I able to see it as a gift . . . Every trial and tribulation has led me to this point in time where I can use my experiences to help other people heal their shadows and find their purpose. It's my sincerest wish that my story will help you embrace your talents and passions, and forge your own path to find your light and soul purpose.

The information and tools I've provided in this book will support you for a long time to come. I envisage you using this book time and time again to self-assess your chakras, undertake the activities to nourish your individual chakras and balance your chakra system through my Chakra Cleanse Meditation.

As you continue with this work, you'll likely experience new challenges. Some days you may feel more blocked than others, but it is not a sign that you're doing something wrong. It's natural that sometimes it may feel harder to find your light, and some days it may feel easier. Working on your chakras and doing the Chakra Cleanse Meditation will take determination and patience. But hang in there! With time, you'll become a master at cleansing and balancing your chakras! (Though, if you're still struggling I've outlined a few of the common challenges people face in the Q & A on page 265.)

The most important thing is to embrace your triumphs and successes. Just stay committed to yourself and you *will* keep moving forward, getting stronger and more luminous, both in your chakras and in your spiritual and intuitive abilities.

Remember: The key to thriving and having an amazing life – vibrant health, abundance, great relationships, a fulfilling career and boundless creativity – is to change your energy by changing your chakras. *This is the way to the light and love.*

Q & A

As I travel the world sharing my story and my work with the chakras, there are questions I'm asked again and again. Here I've included the most frequently asked questions along with my answers, divided by topic area.

I hope this section will help expand your understanding of how you can change your energy and change your life.

I've been doing the Chakra Cleanse Meditation for five months now and I love it. It has certainly brought me more peace and purpose! My life has become calmer, my health has improved, I feel much clearer and my marriage problems have sorted themselves out. But I'm still struggling with focus ... When I bring my awareness to each one of my chakra points, my awareness jumps away. I can only manage to hold my awareness on each one of the chakra points for a short period of time before thoughts come rushing in. I find this frustrating and it makes me feel like I'll never be able to chakra cleanse properly. What can I do?

It's perfectly normal and natural that you can't focus on each chakra point without thoughts coming into your mind . . . Even those of us who have been meditating for a long time have this problem. But rest assured that you are chakra cleansing properly. Otherwise you wouldn't have had these shifts in your life.

When your awareness jumps away from the chakra point and you find yourself thinking or lost in thought again, simply (and calmly) bring your awareness back to the chakra point. And if it jumps away again, simply bring it back again. Just keep coming back to focusing on the chakra point. Don't get frustrated; just refocus. You may still go back and forth between focus and thought for some time. However, your brain will become trained to always come back and focus on the chakra points. Eventually you will find yourself more and more able to focus with less and less stress.

My lower chakras are weak. When I do the Chakra Cleanse Meditation I find it hard to hold my focus on my base, sacral and solar plexus chakras. I can't feel or sense these chakras properly. Does this mean they are weak? I can feel my heart, throat and third eye chakras more strongly, but my lower ones seem non-existent.

Yes, this is a sign that these chakras are weak. When a chakra is weak, many people have the experience that they can't feel it. It seems to not be there.

But we can also experience weak chakras as feeling like they are stagnant, sad or flat, or tight and constricted. When you begin to cleanse your chakras regularly, you'll grow in awareness and will begin to sense and know the state of your chakras. This is the beginning of you developing your skills as an intuitive!

So keep it up. Just keep working on your chakras (paying particular attention to your lower ones) and you'll soon sense them growing and becoming stronger and more resilient.

When I do your guided Chakra Cleanse Meditation, I find myself wanting to spend more time on each chakra. Though your voice is already guiding me on to the next chakra, I intuitively feel I want to stay at the chakra I'm working on. Can I do this?

Yes, of course, and this is what you should do! My guided chakra cleanse was designed as a beginner's tool – a way to have guidance and support when you first learn to work with your chakras. In time you should try to cleanse and balance them yourself because, as you've already found, each of your chakras has different needs.

You'll find that your stronger chakras need less attention and that your weaker ones need more. Cleanse and balance your chakras at your own pace, simply moving up to the next chakra and beginning to work with it when you intuitively sense or feel that the chakra you are working on is 'done' and the next one is ready to go.

Thank you for the extra tips for strengthening weak chakras. These have been really helpful because I have a very weak chakra 1 and chakra 3. I do the Chakra Cleanse Meditation every day and I also make sure I do good things for my base and solar plexus, like getting out into nature and 'standing my ground'. But would you recommend that I focus on strengthening one chakra at a time, or do them together?

I recommend that you begin with your base chakra and focus your attention on strengthening it, and then when that is strong, focus on your solar plexus chakra. It's always best to work from the bottom up – to get your base chakra fit first. Your base chakra is the platform, the springboard of your life and spiritual development, and if it's not working properly this impacts all your chakras.

So start with the base chakra and work your way up. You want your energetic foundation, the base chakra, to be strong and fit and able to funnel the energy up into your higher chakras and down into the earth.

I've been doing the Chakra Cleanse Meditation for three weeks now and I still can't feel my chakras. Does that mean that they are all weak? Or does it mean that I haven't yet developed the intuitive skill to sense them?

If you can't feel *any* of your chakras, it's most likely that you haven't yet developed the intuitive skill to sense them. This will develop in time, so please don't worry about it. But it is important to know that sensing the state of your chakras – whether they are strong or weak – is not a prerequisite for the

Chakra Cleanse Meditation. You don't need to know the state of your chakras in order to heal them.

The most important thing is to work on your chakras and get into a regular habit of chakra cleansing. The rest flows from this.

How long do I need to work on my chakras before I get results?

That depends entirely on you and how often you do the Chakra Cleanse Meditation, and if you complete the meditation or not.

If you do the entire Chakra Cleanse Meditation two to three times a week for six weeks, you will see changes in your life. You will become calmer, clearer, healthier, more focused and aware. But the key to success is sticking with it and making chakra cleansing a regular, lifelong habit.

How can I help my children with their chakras? Can they do the Chakra Cleanse Meditation?

Yes, they can, and many children do. There are children as young as seven who use the Chakra Cleanse Meditation! But for younger children or other children who struggle to do this, you can best help them by helping yourself. The more you work on your chakras, the stronger they become, which in turn helps and supports your child and their chakras. Until the age of seven, children are energetically attached and connected to us; they protect their energy fields through ours.

Should I stop taking my medication and work on my chakras instead?

No, you shouldn't. You should chakra cleanse *in tandem* with taking your medication, and when your health begins to improve, you should speak with your doctor or healthcare practitioner about the next steps.

Can I chakra cleanse when I'm pregnant?

Absolutely. What a wonderful way to support yourself and your baby during this precious time!

When you work on your chakras, you balance yourself and create a strong and luminous energy field. This not only helps you through your pregnancy and birth, it also gives your baby energy and light. I can't think of a more wonderful way to look after your child while it's in utero.

When I chakra cleanse, I fall asleep. Why is this happening? Am I doing something wrong?

This happens to many people when they first start out. It happened to me too. I would become so drowsy I could no longer keep my eyes open, and I'd fall asleep.

When you do the Chakra Cleanse Meditation, you are rapidly opening up and healing your chakras. They are being activated and you are healing your deepest blockages. This is a big job; it can be taxing and make us want to sleep.

Many of us feel sleepy because our shadow – our ego – is resisting the work. It is creating subconscious blockages (drowsiness, sleepiness) to stop us. Your ego benefits from you *not* meditating. When you have blockages in your chakras and aren't connected to the present moment, the ego 'runs the show'. Your shadow is in charge, so to speak, and resists when you begin to heal it and bring light into your energy field. That's why you become sleepy or drowsy.

To prevent this, make sure you sit or stand to do the Chakra Cleanse Meditation. If you lie down, you'll likely fall asleep. And when you're asleep, you can't cleanse and balance your chakras.

Why do we channel the pure light down into our energy fields? Why don't we channel it from the ground up?

The natural flow of the pure light is from heaven to earth. There are two energy flow systems in the body: earth-to-heaven and heaven-to-earth. When we start at the base chakra and work our way up, we foster the earth-to-heaven energy flow system. And when we work with the pure light, we start at the crown chakra and work our way down, working with the heaven-to-earth energy flow system.

I've heard other people talk about the twelve-chakra energy system. But they talk about it in a different way than you do. Why are there different interpretations of it, and how can I know who is right?

I don't know why there are different interpretations of the twelve chakras, and I find this situation unfortunate, as it creates confusion. It would be so much easier if we all perceived the same thing.

The way I see the chakras – starting from the base chakra and ending at chakra 12, with each chakra on top of the other, ascending into the heavens – is the way I've always psychically perceived them. Since I was a child I've seen the chakras this way. (Obviously back then I didn't know they were called chakras, but I always saw them this way.)

Around the year 2000, I started to become aware of the five higher chakras. I could see them in people's energy fields. I then began to earnestly study them. At the time I had never heard anyone else talk about twelve chakras, including the five higher ones. I began calling them the five higher cosmic chakras, and since my enlightened moment in 2007, I have spent many hours working with these chakras.

I can't answer your question about how to know who is right and who isn't. The only guidance I can give you is to follow what you *feel* is right; what feels like your truth.

How is the ego different from the shadow? Or is it the same thing?

Your ego is your shadow. It's the shadow cast by the light of your soul. I sometimes use the word 'ego' to describe our past and our pain and suffering, but mostly I use the word 'shadow'. The two are interchangeable.

In your medical intuition sessions you tell people all about what is wrong with them. You tell them about their past lives and childhood; you talk about what happened in their past and how it's affected them. But it's my understanding that spirituality teaches us to let go of the past and focus our attention fully in the present moment. I've also heard you say that you

don't need to know what is wrong with you for you to heal your life. Can you please explain this contradiction?

It is true that you don't need to know what is wrong with you or what happened to you in the past for you to heal your life. Many people spend a lot of time analysing and digging up the past in the hope they will discover something that will take away their problems of the present. But this approach is futile. It's through healing our shadow and embracing the light within ourselves that we heal our life. And those things about ourselves or our past that we need to know (because they aid our spiritual growth), we'll know.

I told people in my medical intuition sessions about their past-life patterns and childhood hurts because I found that it enabled them to *deeply* accept their shadow.

When I told them the reasons *why* they were feeling a certain way, or why they'd become a certain way, or why they were afraid of or drawn to certain things, it helped them make sense of themselves and their lives. It gave them an 'aha' moment. They were then more easily able to accept themselves, and acceptance is the first step to healing: Accept what is, and then you can radically shift it.

I could completely relate to your story about being an empath. I am sensitive too, and pick up other people's feelings and thoughts. I feel drained and pulled down by other people. How can I protect myself?

Shielding your energy field by engaging your solar plexus chakra is the quickest and easiest way to protect your energy.

Of course, keeping your chakras fit and healthy by doing the Chakra Cleanse Meditation also protects your energy, but the most important thing to do is *not* to worry about protecting your energy field.

When we worry about whether our energy is being protected, we become fearful. Fear makes our chakras constrict, which stops chi (light) from flowing into our energy field, making us less resilient and strong. The best way to protect our energy is to not be afraid.

It is a popular belief in the self-help and spiritual movement that in order to protect ourselves, we need to 'disconnect'. We're encouraged to visualise ourselves in a protective bubble, or 'cutting cords' that are connecting us to others, or to close down some of our chakras or pray for protection. All of this is detrimental and unnecessary, and usually carries with it an undercurrent of fear. (The fear-based thought of: I need to protect myself against others because they could harm me.)

If fear is the reason *why* you are protecting yourself, it doesn't matter what technique you apply, you will simply attract more fear. (More people will steal your energy or you will become more fearful of people stealing your energy.) The most powerful way to protect your energy field is by being powerful! It's by looking after your chakras and shielding. This way you become a *conduit* of love and light. You not only become luminous and immune to the negative psychic energy of others, you also act as a catalytic force.

Don't shut down and be fearful. Open up and spread the light!

In your story you talk about discovering that you are different things: a psychic, an empath, a sensitive, an intuitive, a medium, a ghost whisperer and a truth-teller. Can you please explain what these different things mean?

A psychic is a clairvoyant, someone who has 'clear vision'. We perceive and interpret energy and information by receiving visions and images through our mind's eye.

An empath is clairsentient, someone who has 'clear feeling'. We perceive and interpret energy and information through receiving feelings and emotions. Oftentimes we know how other people feel by feeling it in our own bodies. We are also often highly attuned to people's shadows and the shadow and darkness in the world. (Clairsentience is sometimes referred to as clairempathy.)

A sensitive and an intuitive refers to someone who is sensitive to the psychic and spirit realms and can detect and often interpret their meanings. A sensitive person is mostly clairsentient (clairempathic), and can be some or all of the following: clairvoyant; clairaudient ('clear hearing' – perceives and interprets energy and information through hearing); clairscent ('clear scent' – perceives and interprets energy and information via smell); clairtangency ('clear touching' – perceives and interprets energy and information through touching) and clairgustance ('clear tasting' – perceives energy and information through psychically 'tasting').

I have very heightened senses and have the ability to see, feel, hear, touch and taste energy and information, but I predominately use clairvoyance and clairaudience.

A medium is someone with the ability – through any of the 'clair senses' mentioned above – to connect to and communicate with spirits; with people who had lived on earth and are now back home on the Other Side.

A ghost whisperer is someone who has the ability – through any of the 'clair senses' mentioned above – to connect to and communicate with ghosts; with people who have lived on earth and are still stuck or trapped on the earth plane.

A truth-teller is someone who can see through the layers and masks of the ego to what lies beneath. Truth-tellers want to get to the heart and soul of things; they want to understand and illuminate the truth. They feel called to bust myths and challenge clichés and generalisations. They don't feel comfortable living within the status quo.

How can I become more psychic? I want to be more clairvoyant. I already sense things, so I'm clairsentient, but I want to see much more.

Many people ask me how to become more clairvoyant. They want to have visions and see images and symbols in their mind's eye because they believe that clairvoyance is the 'true' and 'right' measure of a psychic or sensitive person. But you can be very, very intuitive and not be clairvoyant. You can derive a lot of very accurate information without *seeing* anything.

Many people want to be able to 'see'; they want to have visions and images in their mind's eye. But clairvoyance, for many people, is not the most accurate or reliable clair sense.

People who are clairvoyant tend to rely on clairaudience as well as clairsentience to know how to interpret the energy and information they receive.

It is my experience that the most accurate sense is clairsentience. And it's also my experience that the most accurate and gifted intuitives are the ones who use clairsentience as well as some or all of the other clair senses to derive their information. If you want to become an excellent psychic and intuitive, train your senses. Find out first which one (or ones) of your clair senses is dominant; when you receive 'information', what form does it come in? Feeling, hearing, sight? Then train your secondary (weaker) senses to make them stronger. You can do this by spending a week at a time on each one of your secondary senses and exploring the world through them. For example, if clairaudience is a secondary sense, when you're out and about in the world or in meditation, focus only on what you can hear. Block out all the other senses and focus on hearing only. Next, do the same for clairgustance. When you're interacting with people or in meditation, try to 'taste' how the world around you tastes. Of course, you aren't literally putting things into your mouth – you're psychically tasting the world around you . . . You'll be surprised how much information you receive this way.

Often, to get an accurate understanding or diagnosis of a problem or ailment, I would use clairgustance (or clairscent). Then I could usually detect whether it was bacterial or fungal, etc., or what vitamins and minerals were lacking in someone's blood or body.

It's my understanding that if our sixth chakra is open and working properly that we can all be intuitive. But I doubt that is the case with me. I'm a Muggle; I never see or hear anything ... I've been to numerous psychic development classes over the years, but nothing happens, ever. I'm always left feeling frustrated and sad because everyone else gets these amazing visions and receives these amazing messages, but it never happens for me. Are you sure that when I work on my lower chakras, enabling the energy to rise into my chakras 6 and 7, that I too will become intuitive?

Yes, you will. When chakras 1 to 5 are strong enough and energy can easily flow into your chakras 6 and 7, you will become intuitive. This happens because you're energetically designed this way; to be 'open' and sensitive. But when chakras 6 and 7 become activated, that doesn't necessarily mean you'll become clairvoyant. It does mean that one or some of your clair senses will become activated and that you too will be able to perceive and interpret energy and information.

However, many people who claim to be 'Muggles' or 'not psychic at all' often do sense things strongly. They are usually clairsentient, but because they don't realise this is an intuitive sense (and usually the most reliable), they disregard it.

Yes, this is true! I do sense a lot but I didn't think that meant I was open and intuitive. Now I know I am!

Yes, and if you want to develop your clair senses further, train them (in the way I mentioned before). And you never know – your senses of clairvoyance and clairaudience may develop and you'll be able to see visions and hear messages as well.

Can you tell me more about how drugs can open you up and make you more psychic? You had a scary experience with LSD, but I know people who have done ayahuasca and it really helped them become more psychic. Do you think taking drugs would help me?

I think one needs to be cautious about taking drugs for this reason. Personally, I don't think it's necessary for most people. You are energetically designed to be intuitive, so all you need to do is get chakras 1 to 5 fit and healthy and chakras 6 and 7 will naturally (and gently) open up. I also know many people (and have worked with many people) who have taken drugs or plant medicines to open up and experienced negative consequences. The substances have opened them up too quickly and they couldn't handle it, or experienced psychic blowout because of it. However, under the right circumstances – with the right person or shaman or guide – it can be helpful.

You mean like the story of Adam (Samuel's son), who raised his energy too quickly into his chakras 6 and 7 and became unstable?

Yes. Adam's energy field became severely imbalanced because his lower chakras weren't strong enough to hold the amount of energy being poured into his higher chakras. Although his case is extreme – most people don't suddenly become unstable – people do often feel that they can't cope. They feel ungrounded, detached from reality and too 'plugged in'; they can't handle their newfound abilities.

It is much easier and safer to follow the route nature intended for us: cleansing and strengthening our lower chakras so that the energy can naturally rise into the higher chakras.

You mention that there is a correlation between sudden hormonal changes and a spike in psychic/intuitive abilities. Can you speak more about this?

Studies in psychic and supernatural phenomena have shown that there is a marked increase in poltergeist and spirit activity in homes or areas when a child who is intuitively gifted goes through puberty. For some reason, puberty seems to 'charge' or strengthen the abilities and powers of both the intuitive and spirit. Why this is, I don't know. When I went through puberty, my psychic sense suddenly became much stronger, almost overnight.

Women have told me the same about menopause: they suddenly find themselves much more open and intuitive.

Are you psychic about yourself? Can you look inside yourself and see what health problems you have? Can you do this with your own family?

Yes and no. Mostly, I'm not psychic about myself because I'm not objective. I have fears and hopes and dreams, and this makes me 'attached'. When we're attached, our judgement is cloudy and we don't see things the way they really are. Through working on my chakras, though, I've become more objective, and more detached as a result. So, yes, I do see things and know things about myself and my family that one would call 'psychic knowings'.

I feel scared about opening up to my psychic and intuitive sensibilities. How can I make sure I don't see ghosts like you? I want to see angels and energy fields and chakras, but I don't want to see bad things or pick up bad energies.

You can't have one without the other. You can't choose what you wish to see and don't wish to see. It doesn't work like that.

When you open up, you begin to see the world as it really is; how it's made up of light and dark. You also begin to see the many levels of vibration within our world, as well as the spirit beings and entities that inhabit them. Opening your chakras means expanding your limited perception so that you can see the truth: Here on earth and in the spirit realms there are higher and lower vibrations. As above, so below. However, you can protect yourself from having your energy drained or brought down by lesser-evolved beings and ghosts by having a strong and luminous energy field. You'll remember from my story that this was the way the ghost hauntings – as well as me being an over-sensitive empath – stopped. I still saw ghosts (because ghosts are real), but they didn't affect me anymore. Don't be afraid of what you see. They are there anyway, so why fear them?

I see ghosts but I'm afraid. I saw them when I was a child and it was terrifying. It has taken me many years to be able to sleep at night without having the light on. Now I know that they are people who are suffering, people who can't find the light, I feel bad for them. I want to help but I'm so afraid.

I understand your fear of ghosts. I have met very few people who aren't afraid of them, and that's because ghosts (or the idea of ghosts) drives right to the heart of our core fears of vulnerability and safety. Most people see ghosts when they are in bed at night. This isn't because ghosts come prowling after us then — ghosts are always there, night and day — but in the night-time, when it's dark, we have less stimulus and mental activity and are naturally more attuned to the subconscious and psychic part of ourselves. This enables us to see and sense more . . . Many of us also had scary experiences when we were children and we either didn't tell anyone about it because we were afraid they'd think we were crazy, or we *did* tell someone about it and they told us we were making it up. So speaking about ghosts and the paranormal triggers deep fears in most people, and many people aren't willing to look at these fears and overcome them. They would rather pretend ghosts don't exist, or hope that they don't see them.

But ghosts exist, and our fear and rejection of them only perpetuates the cycle. The more we fear death and ghosts, the less we're able to help people find the light after death.

But — as I said before — I don't recommend that you work with ghosts directly. Don't try to communicate with them or engage them in discussion. Work on your own energy field; get it luminous and strong. Then your light will help them find the light.

My son says that he sees things at night in his bedroom. He says there are shadows and dark things floating above him or hovering near the ceiling. He often comes into our bedroom at night, but my husband says he needs to learn to sleep in his own room. But after hearing your story, I'm worried that he might be seeing ghosts. What should I do?

Many children see ghosts, so yes, he may be seeing them. But it doesn't matter whether they are really there or if he is *creating* them to be there. Children have vivid imaginations. I've experienced this many times with my daughter and other small children: when they watch a movie or read a book – about dinosaurs or witches or monsters, for example – they tell me they're scared of seeing these things in their room, or that they are seeing these things in their room. Of course, that's their imagination, but then there are times when they *are* seeing something – dark shapes or figures of spirits or animals, and so on. In both cases, it's best to respond in the same manner: listen to your child so that they feel seen and heard, and make sure you aren't, through your own fear, making them feel afraid. The most important thing is to validate your child's experience by making them feel safe. The second most important thing is to work on your chakras to overcome your own fear.

Reading about your experience of being exorcised was chilling. My question is, how do you feel about the Christian church now? And do you believe that people can become possessed and need to be exorcised?

I have no resentment or anger towards the pastor or the Christian church. Being exorcised was one of the most traumatic and terrifying experiences I've had, but nowadays I see it as my greatest gift. People often say they find my approach to spirituality, the paranormal and life in general *fearless and brave*, but when you've experienced what I have, when you've learned that our fear of things only increases fear in our lives, you learn to face your fears head on and overcome them.

I've lived too much of my life in fear. I want to stay free of it. Yes, people can get possessed. This is not something that most people want to hear; most people want me to tell them that it's untrue and an urban legend, but unfortunately possession is real. However, it doesn't occur often, and when it does – when a ghost or entity fully takes over a person's psyche – the exorcism doesn't need to be as traumatic as they often are. The person conducting the exorcism shouldn't try to rip or pull ghosts out of people and then force them away. It can be done with gentleness and kindness, so that the ghost or entity possessing the person can find the light, and so that the one who was possessed doesn't have to undergo such a psychologically, psychically and physically traumatic ordeal.

It makes me sad that we are taught to fear ghosts. They are portrayed in Hollywood films as malevolent and destructive; you rarely see them as being lonely or frightened. Should we be wary of them? Or can we talk to them and try to help them?

The ghosts you see in the Hollywood films are mostly poltergeists. Angry and malevolent poltergeists only make up a fraction of the ghost population. Also, I was born a ghost whisperer and very psychic (too psychic), so what happened to me in my childhood was unusual. Although many children *do* see ghosts, most don't get harassed by them the way I did.

Even so, it's important to know that ghosts are needy, just like anyone who is suffering and trapped and lonely. Because of this, trying to communicate with ghosts and help them can be exhausting. If you're an empath type, you may pick up on their deep suffering, and this isn't pleasant. One needs to learn how to deal with ghosts, otherwise the experience can be unsettling. This is often why people are afraid of ghosts; because they have had an encounter with them and intuitively picked up on their suffering, which has scared them.

That's why the best way to help ghosts is by creating your own luminous and powerful energy. When the light shines through you, it shines to them. So instead of trying to speak to or engage with ghosts, simply work on your own chakras!

RESOURCES

Here are some additional resources I recommend to support your spiritual practice and journey:

Anatomy of the Spirit, Caroline Myss

The Power of Now, Eckhart Tolle

The Seven Spiritual Laws of Success, Deepak Chopra

Key to Yourself, Venice Bloodworth

ACKNOWLEDGEMENTS

My heartfelt thanks to all who have loved, supported and shared this journey with me (in this world and in the next).

NOTES

NOTES

NOTES

NOTES

NOTES

NOTES